AFRICAN ETHNOGRAPHIC STUDIES OF THE 20TH CENTURY

Volume 67

CHOPI MUSICIANS

CHOPI MUSICIANS
Their Music, Poetry, and Instruments

HUGH TRACEY

Routledge
Taylor & Francis Group

LONDON AND NEW YORK

First published in 1970 by Oxford University Press for the International African Institute.

This edition first published in 2018
by Routledge
2 Park Square, Milton Park, Abingdon, Oxon OX14 4RN

and by Routledge
711 Third Avenue, New York, NY 10017

Routledge is an imprint of the Taylor & Francis Group, an informa business

© 1970 International African Institute

All rights reserved. No part of this book may be reprinted or reproduced or utilised in any form or by any electronic, mechanical, or other means, now known or hereafter invented, including photocopying and recording, or in any information storage or retrieval system, without permission in writing from the publishers.

Trademark notice: Product or corporate names may be trademarks or registered trademarks, and are used only for identification and explanation without intent to infringe.

British Library Cataloguing in Publication Data
A catalogue record for this book is available from the British Library

ISBN: 978-0-8153-8713-8 (Set)
ISBN: 978-0-429-48813-9 (Set) (ebk)
ISBN: 978-1-138-59877-5 (Volume 67) (hbk)
ISBN: 978-0-429-48604-3 (Volume 67) (ebk)

Publisher's Note
The publisher has gone to great lengths to ensure the quality of this reprint but points out that some imperfections in the original copies may be apparent.

Disclaimer
The publisher has made every effort to trace copyright holders and would welcome correspondence from those they have been unable to trace.

Due to modern production methods, it has not been possible to reproduce the fold-out maps within the book. Please visit www.routledge.com to view them.

THE SIX CHOPI MUSICIANS WHO CAME TO DURBAN

Front Row (left to right) Sekelani (Cilanzane, Treble Timbila), Katini (Sange, Alto Timbila), Gomukomu (Sange, Alto Timbila)
Second Row Madoshimani (Debiinda, Bass Timbila), Bokisi (Sange, Alto Timbila)
Behind Majanyana (Gulu, Double Bass Timbila)

CHOPI MUSICIANS

Their Music, Poetry, and Instruments

HUGH TRACEY

Published for the
INTERNATIONAL AFRICAN INSTITUTE
by OXFORD UNIVERSITY PRESS
LONDON NEW YORK TORONTO
1970

Oxford University Press, Ely House, London W. 1

GLASGOW NEW YORK TORONTO MELBOURNE WELLINGTON
CAPE TOWN SALISBURY IBADAN NAIROBI DAR ES SALAAM LUSAKA ADDIS ABABA
BOMBAY CALCUTTA MADRAS KARACHI LAHORE DACCA
KUALA LUMPUR SINGAPORE HONG KONG TOKYO

SBN 19 724182 4

© International African Institute 1970

First published 1948
Reprinted, with a new Introduction, 1970

PRINTED IN GREAT BRITAIN BY OFFSET LITHOGRAPHY BY
BILLING AND SONS LTD., GUILDFORD AND LONDON

TO
KATINI weNYAMOMBE and
GOMUKOMU weSIMBI

INTRODUCTION TO THE SECOND IMPRESSION

In the past twenty-one years since this book was first published, the Chopi have sprung from relative obscurity to world-wide recognition, largely on account of the excellence of their musicianship. The phonographic records which I have been able to publish through the International Library of African Music have established their position as one of the leading, if not the most advanced groups of instrumentalists on the African continent. They compose and perform their distinctive music and dances with undiminished enthusiasm and pleasure, in spite of the gradually changing circumstances which surround them, untouched by compromise with foreign styles and unsullied by the crescendo of popular urban music which has already undermined so much of African musical genius elsewhere.

The fertility of their craft is demonstrated by the fact that not a single composition which I recorded in their villages in the 1940s is still in current use, all the music heard today having been composed afresh in a continuous cycle of rejuvenation. The secret lies not only in their innate musicality but also in the fact that their compositions observe the strict rules of a well-founded technique and the use of an ideal minor tone scale which all Chopi musicians can follow instinctively. They base their music upon what Stravinsky has described as 'the resisting foundation' of an established discipline which allows the greatest freedom of individuality within a clear-cut set of rules. That Chopi music still evokes exultation after at least four centuries is proof enough of its lasting merit as an effective art and recreation for their community.

It is not written music. All of it is created, performed and handed on entirely by aural contact. It is doubtful whether any Chopi musician of the present day, with two or three exceptions, would benefit from a written score. However, future composers, understanding the 'mechanics' of their music from a scientific or measured angle, may yet rise to greater musical heights and bring the art of *timbila* xylophone playing to the notice of a yet wider public of African and world-wide musical intelligentsia.

There are few modifications which need be made in the text, which remains a fair portrayal of Chopi music today, and, of course, with continued acquaintance over the years new details are being added to our knowledge, particularly of the *timbila* maker's craft. For example, only recently I learned that they prefer to cut down dead trees of the *mwenje* rather than the green tree, as otherwise they are liable to have difficulty in curing the wood which is then inclined to crack and have a shorter musical life.

The greatest advance will undoubtedly come when the structure of the music is sufficiently understood to be written down in some adequate notation and played by non-Chopi as well as by the perpetuators of this style.

My son Andrew, who was a small boy when I wrote this book, has begun not only to make *timbila*, but also to play them with the Chopi. He has rewritten the example of one of Gomukomu's tunes *Lavarani micanga sika timbila tamakono*, published in the first edition, in the light of inside knowledge as a player rather than that of an observer only. This replaces the earlier transcription in Appendix V.

PREFACE

A SHORT holiday in Lourenço Marques and the kindness of Portuguese friends there first guided my feet, or more accurately my car, a hundred and fifty miles beyond into the country of the Chopi people. That was in 1940. I was delighted and astonished at what I found in the music of two small orchestras, one at Manhiça and the other beyond the Limpopo at Zandamela. I searched the libraries, perhaps too hopefully, for information upon so musical a people. I was now astonished at what I did not find. Apart from a few paragraphs here and there describing their instruments and a nibble at one or two songs, more particularly by the Junods, father and son, there was nothing whatever to reveal the extent and meaning of Chopi music, poetry, and dancing.

A Portuguese violinist, Sn. Belo Marques, at the Radio Clube of Lourenço Marques, had taken down and set for strings a few of their melodies. But his work, he told me, was essentially for European enjoyment and did not pretend to be a survey.

In the face of this void there was nothing for it but to go and find out for myself. So, each year since then, I have devoted most of my holidays from official duties to visiting those areas where the Chopi are to be found, and taking notes in the hope of learning all I could before eventually making gramophone records. The war years have held up recordings, so the notes hastily written in Chopi villages and in the mine compounds form the basis of this study. The work is far from complete, but may give some indication of the extent and nature of the outcrop of a musical reef which awaits development. From what I have already heard, I am convinced that investigation and recording of Chopi orchestral music will lead to the still greater enrichment of the Chopi themselves, the Bantu people in general, and, indeed, musicians everywhere.

ACKNOWLEDGEMENTS

MY sincere acknowledgements and thanks are due to a number of friends in Portuguese East Africa and South Africa. Without their kindness and assistance this preliminary work could not have been carried out. I would particularly mention Dr. Luiz de Vasconcelos, Administrador of the Zavala District, and his wife Senhora Donna Adelina de Vasconcelos, for their delightful hospitality; Captain Furtado Montanha, Chief Native Commissioner, with Captain Antonio Figueiredo and Lt. Caetano de Carvalho Montez, of the Statistical Department, for many courtesies in Lourenço Marques, and several other Portuguese officials who struggled with my problems and lack of Portuguese; Mr. M. F. Blunt, Consul for Portugal in Durban; Mr. Eric Gallo and the Rev. H. P. Junod, for much encouragement; the many officials of the Transvaal Chamber of Mines who put their facilities at my disposal; and several Compound Managers, particularly Mr. L. G. Hallett of the C.M.R. Mines. There are many others who also enjoyed the music and lent a hand. I would like to mention them all, but they would be the first to protest that this page would look too much like a directory.

Finally my thanks and admiration to the Chopi musicians themselves, who, with their Chiefs and headmen, answered my many questions and treated me most hospitably in their villages. Foremost among them is the composer, musician, and craftsman, Katini weNyamombe, of Zavala's village, and the five musicians who accompanied him to Durban—Gomukomu weSimbi, Majanyana weMoyeni, Sekelani weSikisi, Madoshimani weChari, and Bokisi weMingisele.

Lastly my translators, Majanyana who translated from Chopi into Zulu, and K. E. Masinga who accompanied me on one journey into Zavala and translated from Zulu into English.

HUGH TRACEY

DURBAN
SOUTH AFRICA
September 1944

CONTENTS

INTRODUCTION TO THE SECOND IMPRESSION	vii
PREFACE	ix
ACKNOWLEDGEMENTS	x
LIST OF PLATES AND DIAGRAMS	xiii
I. THE MUSIC MAKERS	1
II. THE LYRICS: POETIC JUSTICE	8
(a) Ŋgodo by Katini, 1940	10
(b) Ŋgodo by Katini, 1943	19
(c) Ŋgodo by Gomukomu, 1940	29
(d) Ŋgodo by Gomukomu, 1942/3	39
(e) Ŋgodo by Sauli Ilova, 1941	52
(f) Ŋgodo by Sipingani Likwekwe, 1941	66
(g) Ŋgodo for Juniors, about 1941	76
III. THE DANCERS AND DANCES	84
(a) Ŋgodo by Katini, 1943, at Zavala's Village	89
(b) Ŋgodo by Gomukomu, 1943, at Banguza's Village	97
IV. THE PLAYERS AND THEIR LEADERS	106
V. CHOPI MUSICIANS ON THE RAND	111
VI. TIMBILA: THE XYLOPHONES OF THE CHOPI	118
(a) Description of the Instrument	118
(b) The Tuning of Timbila	121
(c) The Manufacture of Timbila	129
APPENDIXES	
I. EXTRACTS FROM THE LETTERS OF FATHER ANDRÉ FERNANDES	143
II. GLOSSARY OF WORDS AND MUSICAL TERMS	147
(a) Chopi–English, classified	147
(b) English–Chopi, alphabetical	153

APPENDIXES (continued)

    III. LIST OF CHOPI ORCHESTRAS ON THE MINES OF THE WITWATERSRAND 160

    IV. ANALYSIS OF A TYPICAL CHOPI ORCHESTRAL MOVEMENT, *MZENO*, 8TH MOVEMENT OF THE *ŋGODO* BY GOMUKOMU, 1940 161

    V. MUSICAL TRANSCRIPTIONS 165

    VI. TABLATURE OF *MZENO* MOVEMENT . . . 178

BIBLIOGRAPHY 187

INDEX 189

LIST OF PLATES

	The six Chopi musicians who came to Durban .	*frontispiece*	
I.	*a.* Katini weNyamombe, leader of orchestra .	*facing page*	18
	b. Gomukomu weSimbi, leader of orchestra .	,,	18
II.	Four Chopi drums at Nyakutowa's village .	,,	19
III.	*a.* Gomukomu with his *saŋge timbila* .	,,	34
	b. The village *timbila* orchestra .	,,	34
IV.	Ŋgodo of musicians and dancers at Mavila's village .	,,	35
V.	At Chisiko there were two Clowns .	,,	50
VI.	The Rattle Players .	,,	51
VII.	The Dancers leap into their Dance .	,,	66
VIII.	At a Witwatersrand Mine Compound .	,,	67
IX.	The Dance Leader brings in his men .	,,	82
X.	Oh! Here come the fine young men .	,,	83
XI.	*a.* Ingalishi, maker of *timbila* xylophones .	,,	98
	b. Chopi player seated on a hippopotamus skull stool .	,,	98
XII.	Dance in a Witwatersrand Mine Compound .	,,	99
XIII.	*a.* Bulafu weMpambanisa, *timbila* maker .	,,	114
	b. Muchini Ndambuzi, leader of orchestra .	,,	114
XIV.	*a.* Detail of *timbila* with round arc .	,,	115
	b. Malimba Xylophones of the Shangana-Ndau	,,	115
XV.	'The old man is very fond of music' .	,,	146

DIAGRAMS

I.	Orchestra and dancers: *ŋgodo* of Katini (1943) .	*page*	89
II.	Orchestra and dancers: *ŋgodo* of Gomukomu (1943)	,,	97
III.	Range and distribution of notes in Chopi orchestra	,,	120
IV.	Tuning of five orchestras in Zavala District .	,,	125
V.	Chopi scales .	*facing page*	130
VI.	Timbila. *Saŋge* made by Katini Nyamombe .	,,	138
VII.	Details of Katini's *saŋge* .	,,	139

I
THE MUSIC MAKERS

THE Chopi people of Portuguese East Africa[1] are famous for their music. They play large orchestras of xylophones which they call *Timbila*, and their orchestral dances, *Migodo* (sing. *Ŋgodo*), are probably the most advanced example of African artistic endeavour in the southern part of the continent.

The home country of the Chopi is principally the small triangular piece of lake country just east of the mouth of the Limpopo, in the district of Zavala which lies between long. 34–5° E. and lat. 24–5° S. They are also found in the adjoining districts to the east and north and west of Zavala with a small group in the Incomati river valley at Manhiça.

Their orchestras are to be found in every large village. In the Zavala district alone each of the eight more important chiefs has

[1] The Statistical Department at Lourenço Marques supplies these figures for the Chopi people from the latest census returns:

District of Lourenço Marques
Chibuto	26,565
Muchopes	76,230
Manhiça	6,880

District of Inhambane
Homoine	35,475
Inharrime	35,659
Zavala	75,915

256,724

There are many popular spellings of their name, amongst which are: Bachopi, Tchope, Mchopi, Tsopi, Vachopi, Chope, and Muchope. They themselves seem to prefer 'Muchopi'. For the purposes of this work I shall use the root Chopi without prefix or suffix, except in those few translations of poetry which demand otherwise for the sake of euphony.

his own *Ŋgodo* of orchestra and dancers. This word *Ŋgodo* (sometimes *Igodo, Iŋgodo,* or *Mugodo*) means 'the whole show', including both dancers *Basinyi* and players *Waveti*, and their performance.

I first came into contact with Chopi musicians in 1940 and again in 1941. Then in October 1943, after spending a few more weeks in their country, I was able to bring six Chopi musicians from their villages in Zavala across to Durban in South Africa, there to study their work for three months. More recently I have visited several compounds along the Reef near Johannesburg to see Chopi musicians at work on the mines.

There were two well-known composers among the six musicians who came to Durban, Katini and Gomukomu, whose work is widely performed, and two others who also had several compositions to their credit, Madoshimani and Majanyana. Katini is the leader and composer at the kraal of the Paramount Chief Wani Zavala, and Gomukomu holds the same office at the kraal of Filippe we Mudumane Banguza, an important chief whose country, called Mangene, lies along the north-western boundary of the Zavala district. The people of Banguza claim that they are more truly Chopi than those of the Paramount Chief himself who are sometimes accused of speaking the Chopi tongue with a decided *Inembane* (Inhambane) or Tonga accent, gleaned from their neighbours to the east, in the district surrounding the small port of Inhambane near Cape Corrientes.

Their instruments and their songs and dances reflect great credit upon the abilities of the Chopi. When one remembers that not a note of their music has ever been written down, nor has anyone within their experience, they say, written or translated the words of their poems, it is remarkable to find that they compose new *Ŋgodo* with almost unfailing regularity every two years or so. A *Ŋgodo* is an orchestral dance in nine to eleven movements. Each movement is distinctive and separate, and may last from a minute only, as in the case of some of the introductions, up to five or six minutes each. The whole performance takes as a rule about forty-five minutes, depending upon the intricacy of the dancers' routine and the mood of the moment.

A description of how Katini and Gomukomu set about composing a new orchestral dance will show how musically advanced these men are. Both of them say that the first thing they do is to find appropriate words for their song and compose the verses of the lyric before the music. The subject-matter may be gay, sad, or purely documentary. In every case it is highly topical and appropriate to the locality, so much so, in fact, that most of the allusions would be caught only by those in close touch with the villagers and the district. They are often highly critical of those in authority over them, white or black, and to a large degree it may be said that the poems reflect the attitude of the common people towards the conditions of their society. High good humour is a very prominent feature of most of their poems. Sly digs at the pompous, outspoken condemnation of those who neglect their duties, protests against the cruel and overbearing, outcries directed against social injustices as well as philosophy in the face of difficulties, are all to be found in their songs and shared through their music and dancing. Unlike our own dance songs, they are not preoccupied with sex, with the yearnings of 'torch-bearers', or with the raptures of blue birds and sunsets.

One can well imagine the forcefulness of the reprimand conveyed to a wrongdoer when he finds his misdeeds sung about by thirty to forty strapping young men before all the people of the village, or the blow to the pride of an overweening petty official who has to grin and bear it while the young men jeer to music at his pretentiousness. What better sanction could be brought to bear upon those who outrage the ethics of the community than to know that the poets will have you pilloried in their next composition. No law of libel would protect you from the condemnation conveyed by those concerted voices of the whole village set to full orchestra and danced in public for all to revel in.

It is this aspect of African music which has perhaps escaped our notice—that it performs a highly social and cathartic function in a society which has no daily press, no publications, and no stage other than the village yard in which publicly to express its feelings or voice its protests against the rub of the times. It will be realized how important it is to keep open such a channel through which incidents perpetuated for a while in song express symbolically the plethora of similar incidents which gratify, amuse, exasperate, or sadden the common people —community expression through the self-expression of their composers. It might even be regarded as a form of theatre, a non-dramatic beginning to a living theatre in the sense ascribed to it recently by V. S. Pritchett:[1]

'A living theatre is the boasting of a people; people boasting of their delights, their doubts, their wounds, . . . to show off and to be shown off. That is the beginning of a living theatre.'

But perhaps the word 'perpetuate' is too strong for an entirely aural art, because the songs last only a few years and are then replaced by others more topical. Katini, for example, has to his credit, they say, ten or more *Migodo*. These *Migodo* would contain more than a hundred lyrics and yet, to-day, he can only recall with any certainty his last three works, a matter of thirty or so pieces, with odd numbers from some of the others. His hands, he said, had got out of the way of playing them.

Another aspect of Chopi poetry is at first surprising to us—the apparent paradox that even their saddest songs are sung to gay music. Some of the poems are poignant, particularly those lamenting the untimely death of their children or friends, but all of them, grave or gay, are set to lively music. When I asked them why this was so, they explained, 'We must dance our sorrow.' It is a fundamental difference of outlook between us; we, who of recent centuries have forgotten how to symbolize our religious emotions in the dance, and they, for whom the dance means so much more than just a spectacle or a good-time party. It is a means of intense enjoyment through sharing in a common activity and statement. They speak with one voice and move with one spirit by mystical participation in the compelling music. They do not seek to evoke the reflective emotions which we associate with our sentimental ballads composed in some distant theatre land. They seek the trance-like experience of complete participation in music and dance, their own familiar music set to words which convey their own familiar scene in common joy or common grief. So they dance together and share together.

To return to the composer: when he has decided upon the words of his poem, or, in the case of a long poem, the opening verse, he must now find his melody. *Chichopi*, in common with other Bantu languages, is a tone language, and the sounds of the words themselves almost suggest a melodic flow of tones. This is developed rhythmically, as Gilbert and Sullivan did in their

---

[1] V. S. Pritchett, *The Listener*, No. 795, 6 April 1944, 'The Theatre I want.'

light operas, in one or other of the well-defined patterns which characterize their national verse, with clever use of repetition and offset phrases. The verses are not always metrically alike, as one would naturally expect of a tone language, but all bear a family relationship to the prototype lines. As often as not, the final verse sung to the coda is a repeat of the statement or first line of the poem. In this they follow a well-recognized trick of the trade which is exploited so frequently in our own popular songs. The subject-matter of the poem is not necessarily devoted exclusively to one theme or to one event. Often it appears to be a collection of wholly unrelated observations which are found to be not so unrelated as one might think once the situation has been explained —rather like a game of Pelmanism or free association.

The verse and the leitmotive now fixed in the composer's mind, he sits at his instrument, over which his hands wander with expert deftness, and picks out the melody with one of his rubber-headed beaters. After a while, during which his right hand becomes accustomed to the new tune, his left will begin to fill in the harmonies or contra-melody with well-understood sequences, punctuated with rhythmic surprises suggested by the ebb and flow of the words. Now the right hand will wander away from the melody, *mapsui*, into a variation, *kuhambana*, and as he sings the words over to himself the contrapuntal accompaniment will begin to form under his hands. How much of this process is the result of dexterity and habit and how much comes from direct musical inspiration remains to be discovered. At least the orchestral overtures which have no poetry upon which to base their motives must depend upon genuine musical originality.

They now have the *primary* melodic line of the poem—the subject or leitmotive—and the *secondary* melodic accompaniment —the orchestral·sentence—which fits the words contrapuntally, with a number of variations and sequences. It is this secondary melody which becomes the main theme for the orchestral part of the work. From it the orchestral ground is developed by the composer himself and by his fellow musicians as they play. In this degree the composition now becomes communal, with the players of the various pitches of *Timbila* (treble, alto, tenor, bass, and double bass) improvising their own parts to the ground. But they all conform to the master pattern set by the composer who may or may not have composed all these ground variations himself. It is incorrect to think that the performance of such variations is entirely impromptu. It is not. A repetition of the work will elicit the same variations as before, though the number of times they are played will depend upon the number of repeats, *kuvagela*, required by the dancers or the leader. Recordings of their work have elucidated this point.

The composer is now left with the final touches to decide. He must devise an introduction, arrange the general sequence of the movement, and decide how he will complete his coda. The introduction to a movement is often complicated. The leader may first play over a statement of the melody, *kukata indando*. Then after a short pause he will start an intricate cadenza, *kudala*, which leads, via a run down the instrument, *kusumeta*, and an introductory phrase, *kuniŋgeta*, into the full orchestral opening, *kuvetani vootsi*. Other introductions are not so intricate and may sometimes be only a matter of a couple of notes by the leader before the whole orchestra follows. The sequence of the movement is dependent upon the steps to be danced and the verses to be sung. It is arranged later between the composer and his dance leader. This leaves only the coda. Generally, though not always, the coda is a repeat of the first line or verse of the lyric, and the leader must devise a musical indication, *kuvelusa*, which his men will be able to hear and so follow him into the coda.

The musical side is now complete in every essential, but the dance has yet to be composed and fitted to the music. The composer will call on one or two of his friends to help him play over his new work to the dance leader, who listens attentively and devises in his mind the dance routine to fit it. Then, with the plan of action clearly in his mind, the dance leader will try out his new steps and call upon the composer to give him a stipulated number of repeats of the basic sentence or phrase for each part of the dance. Naturally there would be confusion if a clearly devised plan were not strictly adhered to by both dancers and orchestra. But the system works without the writing of a word or note on paper, and between them the whole movement takes shape.

The singing of the words of the lyric is part of the dance routine and is undertaken by the dancers. They sing as a rule in unison with occasional harmonic passages by their leader. The clear statement of the subject and counter-subjects by young male voices set against the percussion accompaniment of the mellow-toned *Timbila* makes stirring music.

So each new movement is added and replaces the old one which is discarded from now on, and in the matter of a few weeks or months the *Ŋgodo* has sloughed its old skin and is born afresh with new words, new music, and new dances.

It is against this highly developed pattern of melody, contra-melody, and action, that Chopi poetry is heard.

From this description it will be seen that the general pattern of Chopi orchestral music has something in common with our own seventeenth-century music and may in fact be described as a type of Chaconne or Passacaglia. They both originated in dances, in our case from Spain and Italy, and in theirs no one knows where, except that many centuries ago they appear to have come from somewhere in central Africa via the famous Kingdom of the Mocaranga.

Percy Scholes in his *Oxford Companion*[1] describes the Chaconne and Passacaglia in detail and then states:

'The keyboard composers of the seventeenth and early eighteenth centuries made great use of this form . . . and fine examples will be found in Frescobaldi, Buxtehude, Couperin, Handel, Bach, and others.

'Lully and then Rameau often ended their operas with a piece in this form. . . .'

He quotes a number of famous pieces of music in this form including the last movement of Bach's D minor Suite and his Passacaglia and Fugue in C minor—considered one of his greatest organ works; the magnificent 'Goldberg' Variations; the Thirty-Two Variations in C minor for piano by Beethoven; and the Finale of the Brahms Fourth Symphony.

'It will then be realised [he writes] that some of the grandest compositions the world has yet had have been based upon the principle of the Chaconne-Passacaglia type of variation.'

With such precedents before them we need not fear for the future of Chopi orchestral music.

---

[1] *Oxford Companion to Music*, Percy A. Scholes, 2nd American Edition, Oxford, p. 150.

II
THE LYRICS: POETIC JUSTICE

THERE is no doubt that our enjoyment of African music is greatly enhanced when we know what the songs are about and the setting from which they spring. It is almost impossible for foreigners to pick up the words of an African song as it is sung. I have not yet met one who could. We have to get the singers to repeat the words to us at dictation speed and then ask them to sing the song over again. It is then much easier to follow. But beginners must be warned that there is a strict routine to be adhered to in this operation or else whole lines will be left out and lyrically important repeats omitted. The singers themselves often have difficulty in remembering exactly what they *do* sing unless they hum the song over to themselves from the beginning and find out just what the words were. But this is not uncommon: we do the same ourselves. It takes time and patience to be certain you have the poetry down correctly. And even when you have your words down as correctly as may be, you find they have taken liberties with them which you will not find in the text-books. Poetic phraseology in the Bantu languages is as distinctive as poetic English or French, for example. The endings of words are particularly liable to slight alteration in song. Consequently, when taking down these Chopi lyrics I have been very careful to write what they sing, or appear to me to sing, and not always what they would say in conversation. Thus a word normally ending in *-a* may frequently be sung as *-e*. Names of persons and places are often so changed. The name of the Paramount Chief *Vani Zavala* may be changed to *Vane Zavale*, and *Chopi* become *Chope*. One is never certain when they will make the alteration and I have made no attempt to standardize. It is a phenomenon shared to my knowledge by both Karanga and

THE LYRICS: POETIC JUSTICE

Zulu people as well. An apparently incorrect suffix in poetry should be heard in song before making too hasty a correction. Locality also has to be remembered, for the singers constantly reminded me of their distinctive dialects.

Errors in word division will, I hope, be excused by linguists, who will note that the material itself is substantially correct.

I must admit here that my knowledge of *Chichopi* is slight, and except for a working knowledge of *Chikaranga* and a little *Isizulu* I have had to rely to a large extent upon my interpreters. Whenever in doubt I checked and cross-checked by asking the same question in different contexts. Musical terms I readily picked up by reference to similar terms in use among the Karanga, but the translation of poetry was a different matter. I have not been able to find a Chopi linguist fluent in English, or a European sufficiently fluent in Chopi, to follow the nuances of poetry unaided by local explanation. Consequently, I offer my translations as an interpretation of the text in the light of those village circumstances which were explained to me at considerable length. I stand under correction if I have misunderstood the situations, but I believe they are materially correct in detail. My explanations of the background of each of the fifty poems contained in these seven *Migodo* may help to place them in their true perspective—on the village dance-floor. As to the English of my translations, I believe in keeping as strictly as possible to the literal wording of the original, but in avoiding at all costs the pseudo-romantic phraseology so commonly used by translators of African stories and songs. It is quite impossible to adhere to the rhythm of the original without artificiality, and that would leave a wholly false impression. The original poems are crisp and full of the most unexpected rhythmic patterns which I find are not suggested at all in cold print, except, perhaps, in the division of the lines and verses. It is easy to divide the verses as they are usually separated by one or two repeats of the motive by the orchestra. But the lines I am not always so certain about; so for lack of any precedents I must needs set my own. The Chopi, of course, have never visualized their songs in print. They only think of them aurally in terms of melody and dance rhythm.

1. ŊGODO

Composed in 1940 by Katini, orchestral leader and composer at the village of Wani Zavala, Zavala District.

MOVEMENTS

1. *Musitso wokata.*	First Orchestral Introduction.
2. *Musitso wembidi.*	Second Orchestral Introduction.
3. *Musitso woraru.*	Third Orchestral Introduction.
4. *Ŋgeniso.*	The Entry of the Dancers.
5. *Mdano.*	The Call of the Dancers.
6. *Joosinya.*	The Dance.
7. *Joosinya cibudo combidi.*	The Second Dance.
8. *Mzeno.*	The Song.
9. *Mabandla.*	The Councillors.
10. *Citoto Ciriri.*	The Dancers' Finale.
11. *Musitso kugwita.*	The Orchestral Finale.

Movements 1, 2, and 3 have no words to them.

4th Movement. ŊGENISO. *The Entry of the Dancers*

Hiŋgawona iŋkupo wamaPortugezi,
MaPortugezi vahanya kumadanda
   Ni tikuku
Cica pondo ciŋgiza.

It is time to pay taxes to the Portuguese,
The Portuguese who eat eggs
   And chicken.
Change that English pound!

The time for paying taxes is naturally a somewhat trying period when the poor unfortunate who is short of cash must find the necessary or take the consequences. The paying of taxes in cash in a country where barter economy is still prevalent makes the parting even more painful than with us. It is an oft-recurring theme in native songs.

The rightness of reference to the Portuguese as those who eat eggs and chicken will be wistfully admitted by every good Portuguese housewife in the district, of whom there may be a dozen or so. (The last census shows a total of 27 Europeans in the Zavala district.) Had they added fish from the lakes as well, the picture of the available choice of proteins would have been complete! But with the memory of my hostess vividly in mind I would gladly return any day to sample again the hundred and one delicious disguises she has conjured up for this culinary trinity.

Apart from the small but ready market for eggs and chicken to the Europeans of the district, the natives themselves, I understand, do not, as a rule, eat eggs. They would all like some beef occasionally, but the district is so wooded that there is insufficient pasture for cattle.

'Change that English pound' has also a mild sting in it. The chief source of revenue for the whole tribe is from the wages earned in the mines of the Rand in South Africa, to which an alarmingly high percentage of their able-bodied men return again and again. There they are paid in South African money, and on return to Moçambique territory there is a certain loss on the exchange, sometimes as much as 2s. in the pound. For their taxes they must present the local currency, the full 100 escudos, which they also call a pound, *pondo*.

5th Movement. MDANO. *The Call of the Dancers*

Kapitini ŋgunevuka.
Ŋgutane mana nyumbani kamina nedisete sopa.
Kapitini ŋgubava mbilo iŋgonda kufuma suŋga Malova niŋgonaca.
Kapitini ŋgunevuka.

Wani ŋgene waCivunye
Atu ŋkoma bakubakwane uniŋgete
Uŋgandapṣuala uleka timbila.
Tsula ucaka nyumba yako.

Utile nimifo yakuwindukela kudawutisa diwafi nimboma Dibuliani
Kapitini unepata ako ninyamai waŋgu ucipeka.
Aŋgonaca?
Mafewani waŋgu kudawa.

Mweno ŋguwapfa wacileŋga.
A tu adiho Cipaupau waMadandani.
Dibuliani mini leŋgako vadihowa vamatiko vacitela kutanigela.
Adiho Fainde.
Minileŋga ako micilamba kuwomba?

Kapitini ŋgunevuka.
Ŋgutane mana nyumbani kamina nedisete sopa.
Kapitini ŋgubava mbilo iŋgonda kufuma suŋga Malova niŋgonaca.
Kapitini ŋgunevuka.

Kapitini, you make trouble.
You find me in my hut having taken cider.
Kapitini, you have only just been made a messenger, yet you send
    Malova to come and catch me.
What have I done?

Kapitini, you make trouble.
Wani, son of Chivune!
BakuBakwane said to me,
'Don't waste your time with *Timbila*,
Go and build your hut.'

You woke up early in the morning to look for your sjambok and
    watch, Dibuliani
Kapitini, you beat both of us, me and my wife.
What have I done?
So my Mashewani died.

I heard them trying to hush it up.
Chipaupau, son of Madandani, was there.
Dibuliani spoke about me in the presence of strangers and they told me.
Even Fainde was there.
Why don't you tell me to my face?

Kapitini, you make trouble.
You find me in my hut having taken cider.
Kapitini, you have only just been made a messenger, yet you send
    Malova to come and catch me.
What have I done?
Kapitini, you make trouble.

This is the outcome of a very unfortunate affair in which there seems to have been some misunderstanding in the village and out of which Katini came second best. It was the time of the cider, that is about November, when the Cazhu trees[1] provide their

---

[1] This remarkable tree is so versatile I quote H. F. Macmillan's description of it in full, from his excellent book. Its local name varies from *Caʒu*, or *Canju*, to *Kadju*.
'*Anacardium Occidentale*.
'Cashew-nut, Cajugaha, Mundirimaram. Anacardiaceae, Mango family.
'A spreading tree, 30–40 feet high, native of Tropical America and West Indies, naturalised in Africa, Ceylon, India, &c. The fruit consists of two distinct parts: (*a*) the large, fleshy, pear-shaped stalk (Cashew-apple), 3–4 inches long, which is juicy and astringently acid; (*b*) the small kidney-shaped, grey or brown nut, about 1–1½ inches long, at the extremity. The latter has an edible kernel, which when roasted has a very agreeable nutty taste and is much relished for dessert. It is in

THE LYRICS: POETIC JUSTICE

abundant fruit for cider-making. The Cazhu nut grows at the tip of the fruit, which is made into a most potent cider to which the whole tribe is addicted. So potent in fact is this cider that the Administrador of the district claims that more than three-quarters of the crime of the year is crowded into this one month.

So in the circumstances, if, as it seems, there had been a misunderstanding of instructions on the part of Katini and the two elders, the season of the year may be partially to blame. Katini, it appears, was making xylophones for the Chief, Wani Zavala, when he received instructions from the messenger, Bakußakwani, that Zavala wanted him to finish his new hut before the rains came on in December or so. So he left his work on the *Timbila* and went on with the hut. Then Kapitini came along and countermanded Bakußakwane's orders, wanting to know why he had not finished the *Timbila*. In point of fact, it is believed that Kapitini was merely throwing his weight around, having only recently been promoted to be a chief's messenger. But bearing a grudge against Katini, he sent two of his minions early one morning to beat him up in his hut while he was still asleep. This was carried out by Malova and Dibuliani, who are said to have injured severely both Katini and Mashewani, his wife, who was sleeping by his side. Mashewani died some five months later, not, they say, from the beating she received; but all the same, Katini, who was devoted to his wife, felt that this painful experience must have shortened her life.

It will be noticed that in the second verse he first calls upon the name of the Paramount Chief as an oath of truthfulness in his witness of the event. The other two mentioned by name as having heard of the intrigue against him, Chipaupau and Fainde, were two fellow musicians and friends of his.

---

demand in Europe, and is exported to some extent from S. India, E. Africa, &c., for use in confectionery and dessert. These "nuts" are generally valued in London at about 30–35s. per cwt., and in Ceylon are retailed at about 1s. 4d. per hundred, shelled. The shell of the nut is acrid and poisonous. All parts of the fruit are of various uses in native medicine. An intoxicating beverage (kaju) is obtained by distillation from the fleshy receptacle (hypocarp) in Mozambique, subject to Government licence. A gum obtained from the tree is obnoxious to insects and is recommended for book-binding. The juice from the incisions made in the bark forms an indelible ink. The tree is especially adapted to moderately dry districts, near the sea, but also thrives up to 3,000 ft. Propagated by seed.'

Extract taken from *Tropical Planting and Gardening*, by H. F. Macmillan, p. 247, published by Macmillan & Co., Limited, St. Martin's Street, London.

6th Movement. JOOSINYA. *The Dance*

> *O—o, hiŋganipwa muteto,*
> *Hiŋganipwa muteto waƱamadje.*
>
> *O—o, hiŋganipwa muteto,*
> *Hiŋganipwa muteto waƱamadje.*
> *Amano waMaʒi wabwakide kupa wati pondo.*
>
> *Amano waMaʒi wabwakide kupa wati pondo.*
> *Mihumbo yaŋgu tata,*
> *Tipondo nati mana hayi?*
>
> *Mihumbo yaŋgu tata,*
> *Tipondo nati mana hayi?*
>
> *O—o, hiŋganipwa muteto,*
> *Hiŋganipwa muteto waƱamadje.*
>
> O—oh, listen to the orders,
> Listen to the orders of the Portuguese.
>
> O—oh, listen to the orders,
> Listen to the orders of the Portuguese.
> Men! The Portuguese say, 'Pay your pound.'
>
> Men! The Portuguese say, 'Pay your pound.'
> This is wonderful, father!
> Where shall I find the pound?
>
> This is wonderful, father!
> Where shall I find the pound?
>
> O—oh, listen to the orders,
> Listen to the orders of the Portuguese.

This is a particularly delightful and light-hearted lyric. The subject is topical and eternal, and it is apparently as great a mystery to them as to us to know where on earth the money is coming from.

It appears from the verse that the Portuguese have one or two nicknames, *Ʊamadje* and *Maʒi*, as well as the more usual *Portugezi*. What their significance may be I do not know and they could not tell me, but most Europeans have a number of names by which they are familiarly known to the native people. The latter name, *Maʒi*, may possibly come from the Karanga *Majishe*, great chief, or it might well be 'the sea people' from *Amanzi*, 'water'.

7th Movement. JOOSINYA CIBUDO COMBI'DI. The Second Dance

Hici O—o,
O—o, ŋgo tawona Mzeno.
Hici O—o,
O—o, ŋgo tawona Mzeno.
Cima ewo wubemba hiwo wonako niMaportugezi wopeka manza nivavasikati Wacawepata nitiŋgamu.
Hici O—o,
O—o, ŋgo tawona Mzeno.
Sing Ho—o,
Ho—o, come and see the Mzeno.
Sing Ho—o,
Ho—o, come and see the Mzeno.
Here is a mystery, the Portuguese beat us on the hands,
Both us and our wives.
Sing Ho—o,
Ho—o, come and see the Mzeno.

Here again is a very light-hearted lyric. The *Mzeno*, of course, is the next movement of the *Ŋgodo* which contains the great song. There is a preliminary dance before the song, so it is quite correct to say come and 'see' rather than 'hear' the *Mzeno*.

It is the local custom for the Portuguese to beat the palms of the hands as a corporal punishment instead of 'the part specially fatted by nature for the sacrifice'. This is naturally somewhat disconcerting to the offenders. But from conversations I have had on the subject there seems to be some resentment that the punishment should be meted out to their womenfolk as well as the men. There are other references in their songs to their dismay that even chiefs are given this punishment, and that their own men, native sepoys at the administrative office, should have to carry out the sentence, which seems to be considered something of an indignity. On the other hand, the giving of lashes can be far more brutal. It is so much a matter of opinion.

8th Movement. MZENO. The Song
Maŋganakana ŋgwera macitala mzinda macidanwa wuSibuyeye.
WuSibuyeye ukukela mzinda acirumwa ŋgwakoma.
Uŋguyaruma Sibuyeye tikoni kaMahafi Biŋgwana?
Macaŋgana asala kunyenyedza.

*Kuye maŋgalwa kawakoma micikhano Katini wabvuka kunasika timbila
    kuleka ŋgodo.*
Mahambane ciwomba nivakoma.
Hiŋgawomba awe Fainda ukalako ucisika timbila.

Cimuke micimona vadikavakoma losani ŋgu 'mbo dia'.
Losani tatinene Cimuke mbolava vakoma kukala ndimane navo.

VaBaŋguzi vahanyote ukoma waMahlaza iŋkumaha vacikolo
VaMaŋgeni vahomide vacigiya
Vapota Mindumane wawe.

Ticimwha ŋgu Mahebane akopṣuala ŋgukona kusela
Vaŋgamaha vakutiye vakoma.

Maŋganakana ŋguvera macitala mzinda macidanwa wuSibuyeye.
WuSibuyeye ukukela mzinda acirumwa ŋguvakoma.
Uŋguyaruma Sibuyeye tikoni kaMahaṣi Biŋgwana?
Macaŋgana asala kunyenyedza.

The elders came very early to the council called by Sibuyeye.
Sibuyeye comes from the council appointed by the Chiefs.
Why do you send Sibuyeye into the country of Mahashi Bingwana?
The Shangaans are detestable.

It was reported to the Chiefs that Katini refuses to play *Timbila* in
    the Dance.
Mahambane told this to the Chiefs.
You ask Fainde if this is true, because he is a player of *Timbila*.

If you come across Chimuke, greet him with a 'Good day'.
Greet him well, because he likes to be in amongst the Chiefs.

Banguza became Chief instead of Madhlaza because he'd been to school.
The people of Mangeni are happy
As they now avenge Mindumane.

This is because Mahebane sat around drinking,
Because Chiefs are vain.

The elders came very early to the council called by Sibuyeye.
Sibuyeye comes from the council appointed by the Chiefs.
Why do you send Sibuyeye into the country of Mahashi Bingwana?
The Shangaans are detestable.

   Sibuyeye was not a Chopi by birth but either a half- or full-blooded Shangaan. The Shangaans live on the other side of the Limpopo river and are not liked by the Chopi. So when Sibuyeye, who had been living among them for many years, was eventually made a chief's messenger, there was a certain amount of resentment at the appointment. Thus when Sibuyeye was sent into the district called Mahashi Bingwana, a small district near the Paramount Chief's own 'country' in which Katini used to live, the composer expressed their indignation that a Shangaan should trespass upon their home ground. This fiercely tribal loyalty is very noticeable in many Bantu people and particularly so in the Zulu. Whether there was another and more personal reason for their objection I could not discover.

The next verse has its background in a period of domestic troubles which fell upon Katini about 1939. He felt that all hands were against him except those of a few of his trusted friends and musicians. This man Mahambane, it appears, had remarked in the presence of Wani Zavala, the Paramount Chief, that Katini was 'off' his music. This remark got back to him and, since his one consuming passion is his music and his instruments, he was naturally indignant, and referred them to Fainde his friend, who would often go to Katini's hut of an evening to play together with him quietly. He was, in point of fact, working upon his new *Ŋgodo*, orchestral dance, and so he used this means to disprove Mahambane's accusation in the most pointed manner possible—in his new composition.

Chimuke, they say, was a previous Administrador, Commissioner of the District. Who he was is not certain, but it appears from what they say that he was a stickler for etiquette, a foible they thought it wise to indulge by a particularly hearty *Mbo dia* or 'Good day'.

The next two verses refer to the deposition of a chief some years ago, and a second deposition which restored the original line of succession. It was like this—though the story is a little involved but I trust correct.

Mindumane was chief of the Mangeni district. He was deposed by the Administrador because he failed in his chieftainly duties. His brother Mahebane was given the chieftainship, but he in turn failed and took to drink. When both brothers had eventually died, the question arose as to whose son should be promoted, the son of the elder or of the younger brother. The Administrador's choice fell upon Filippe Banguza, son of the elder, because among other virtues he had had a good education. The line of succession was thus restored, which was to the common people a satisfactory conclusion.

The reprimand about chiefs who sit around drinking because they are vain seems to be merited, so the Administrador tells me. It has been a matter of some concern to him that the chiefs, who should know better, take advantage of their position not to work for the common good but to indulge themselves. This is a situation which even the poets of the country do not hesitate to publish abroad without fear, and it appears more than once in their songs—literally a kind of poetic justice.

Father André Fernandes in 1560 also had something to say about the failing.[1]

9th Movement. MABANDLA. The Councillors

Atu hawomba,
Heŋgati hecileŋga maleŋgo
Fambanyane alavako wukoma.

Fambanyane akohode iŋkuwona yatiŋgoti kuhokiswa matokwe
Kota onatsanela Manjeŋgwe
Utawa kuyambala ŋganju.

Atu hawomba,
Heŋgati hecileŋga maleŋgo
Fambanyane alavako wukoma.

We are saying,
We have reason to say we believe
Fambanyane would have liked to be Chief.

Fambanyane was brought bound before the judge,
So now he can't threaten Manjengwe.
He has lost his chance of wearing chief's uniform.

We are saying,
We have reason to say we believe
Fambanyane would have liked to be Chief.

This song, which was composed before the tragic death of Manjengwe in Lisbon, is an example of mild political propaganda. Katini as usual was backing his friend Manjengwe, who he hoped would become the Paramount Chief of Zavala in good time, and so wear the green braid. But Fambanyane also claimed to be the heir to the chieftainship, and did so with such violence that he

[1] Appendix I, extracts from pp. 66 and 142.

PLATE I

a. Katini weNyamombe, Leader of the Orchestra at the village of Wani Zavala, the Paramount Chief of the Chopi

b. Gomukomu weSimbi, Leader of the Orchestra at the village of Filipe Banguza, and said to be the best living exponent of the Timbila

PLATE II

Four Chopi Drums, at Nyakutowa's Village

The two on the left are *Ncinga* drums, standing 2' and 2' 7" tall and 10½" and 11½" across the head; the two on the right are *Ιgoma cikulu*. The farther one measures 2' 6" tall and 21" across, and the nearer (the one they had to break the door posts down to get out of the hut) is 3' 9" tall and 26" across the head. This latter is made of Muhomzwa wood, and the other three of Muvangazi

was had up for disturbing the peace. He was taken before the magistrate and sentenced to a term of imprisonment. This blot on his escutcheon put him out of the running, so to speak, and left the field open for Manjengwe.

This mildly sarcastic poem completed the discomfiture of Fambanyane.

10th Movement. CITOTO CIRIRI. The Dancers' Finale
Heŋgisa nzila yaMasava yakuta gelwa Katini ati hantini
Jigaŋgo caCidodo waKambanini katu.
Awe Katini, wacikugela midiho?
O——, hai cava!

We hear a rumour about Masawa told to Katini at his own home,
That she is courted by Chidodo of Kambanini, they say.
'You, Katini; what is the damage?'
'Oh——, that I can't say!'

This delightfully wicked little song is about Masawa, Katini's sister-in-law. She was a widow, and an attractive widow too, by all accounts. Chidodo of Kambanini's kraal was a very ardent admirer of hers but, I gather, was a little slow in making up his mind. In any case, what she did was no concern of Katini; he was not her guardian. So when their names were coupled together Katini disclaimed any hand in the affair, all the time knowing that his song was bound to have the effect of forcing them to make up their minds one way or the other. This situation was explained to me with some amusement, from which I gathered there must have been even more humour in the event than they could very well explain without letting down the merry widow.

11th Movement. MUSITSO KUGWITA. Orchestral Finale

This is a repeat of the first orchestral introduction, the musical statement of the whole work, and contains no poem.

2. ŊGODO

Composed in February 1943 by Katini, orchestral leader and composer at the village of Chief Wani Zavala, Zavala District.

MOVEMENTS

1. *Musitso wokata.*   First Orchestral Introduction.
2. *Musitso wembidi.*   Second Orchestral Introduction.

3. *Ŋgeniso.*	The Entry of the Dancers.
4. *Mdano.*	The Call of the Dancers.
5. *Doosinya.*	The Dance.
6. *Jibudu.*	The Second Dance.
7. *Mzeno.*	The Song.
8. *Mabandla.*	The Councillors.
9. *Njiriri.*	The Dancers' Finale.
10. *Musitso wokata kugwitisa.*	Orchestral Finale.

Movements 1 and 2 are played by the orchestra alone without singers.

3rd Movement. ŊGENISO. *The Entry of the Dancers*

 Ye Dawoti!
 Dawoti tsulai ucagela Madikise.
 Unakugela kubwaka kavaluŋgu vaŋga bala kokwe.
 Citombe unamona Madikise!

 Hey, Dawoti!
 Dawoti go and ask Madikise.
 He will tell you about our grandfathers.
 Chitombe, behold Madikise!

Dawoti was a native clerk in the office of the District Commissioner, Dr. Luiz de Vasconcelos, whose native name is Madikise. He was given this name, which bears the interpretation of 'Lawgiver' or 'Justice', because of his reputation for fair and impartial judgements in his courts. Dawoti, the clerk in the office, acts as a go-between and is the man to be approached when you want to see the District Commissioner (Administrador) upon any matter involving the law, matters of inheritance, and so on. The Administrador has the power to make or depose chiefs, but before doing so he naturally makes detailed inquiries about the rights of succession in their tribal law. During the last few years there had been cause for one or two new chiefs to be established and old ones deposed, hence the allusion to 'our grandfathers', meaning to our tribal customs.

Chitombe is one of the great ancestors of the tribe, a chief of long ago. He may even have been the supposed progenitor of the Chopi people. Invoking his name therefore is natural, like calling upon the name of the tribal god or ancestor, and amounts to a kind of blessing upon the judgement of the Administrador in his court of justice.

THE LYRICS: POETIC JUSTICE

Dawoti, unfortunately, a few months after this song was composed, fell from grace and was dismissed from his post at the office.

4th Movement. MDANO. The Call of the Dancers

 Lavanani ʒentu Zavala,
 Lavanani ʒentu Zavala hica kaMagule.

 Lavanani ʒentu Zavala,
 Lavanani ʒentu Zavala hica kaMagule.

 Mzeno waMadikise
 Ulawa ŋgoŊgundwane kaMagule.

 Bilenimasiyi kunatisa ŋgumasotca ye maGerimani.
 Bilenimasiyi kunatisa ŋgumasotca ye maGeremani.
 Wani wajawula asuŋgako tinemba taukoma.
 Wani wajawula asuŋgako tinemba taukoma.
 Hambuza waManjeŋgwe wasuŋgidwe tinemba taukoma?
 Hambuza waManjeŋgwe wasuŋgidwe tinemba taukoma?

 Lavanani ʒentu Zavala,
 Lavanani ʒentu Zavala hica kaMagule.

 Come, you people of Zavala,
 Come, you people of Zavala, and go to Magule.

 The Song of Madikise,
 It is wanted by Ngundwane at Magule.

 Bilene Macia, there will be a battle with the German soldiers.
 Wani is happy because he is wearing his official uniform!
 But did Manjengwe ever wear the official uniform?

 Come, you people of Zavala,
 Come, you people of Zavala, and go to Magule.[1]

In July 1939 the President of Portugal, President Carmona, visited the colony of Moçambique and toured the country. There were many ceremonies in his honour, amongst them being a grand *indaba* of native peoples on the flat country near the Inkomati river at a place the natives call *Magule*. It is the site of the old battlefield on the road between Macia and Xinavane where the Shangaans under Gungunyana were eventually defeated by the Portuguese, near the lake called Chuali. To this place the Chopi musicians and people were called, together with the other

[1] Translation omitting the repeats of verses.

tribes, and, of course, the Chopi musicians were the chief attraction of the day as they played and danced Katini's *Ŋgodo* with massed orchestra and dancers—over a hundred musicians, it is said, and twice that number of dancers. It is to this function that Katini refers. Zavala (or, more correctly, *Zavala*) is the name of the Paramount Chief of the Chopi people and the district is the Zavala district.

Katini pays a gentle tribute to Madikise, the Administrador, Dr. Luiz de Vasconcelos, by referring to the music they will perform at *Magule*, Magul, as the Song of Madikise, his District Commissioner. Ngundwane is the native name of the previous Administrador of the Zavala district, who was transferred to Bilene, Macia, the district in which the battlefield of Magul is situated, when Madikise took his place. The verse makes it appear that the fellow Administrador had sent over to Madikise to bring along 'his music' for the ceremony.

'There will be a battle with the German soldiers' clearly reflects the feeling of the times with the war in Europe impending. This poem was not performed until the 1943 *Ŋgodo*, though it may have been composed much earlier.

The more important chiefs are given an official uniform by the Portuguese Government of the colony which they are expected to wear upon official occasions. Naturally this important function was one of those times, and Wani, the present Zavala, had put on his uniform with its khaki trousers and tunic decorated with green braid. An embossed staff and wide-brimmed hat complete the outfit. Wani, who is a short man, looks well in his uniform, and his intelligent face with its little black moustache no doubt betrayed the consciousness of this fact.

The reference to Manjengwe is a long story and more fully referred to in the 7th Movement, *Mzeno*. He was a great friend and fellow musician of Katini who died in Lisbon in 1940. He was in direct line of succession for the chieftainship, and Katini felt the loss of Manjengwe very keenly.

5th Movement. DOOSINYA. The Dance

 Aŋga kaMalanje maniruketela miciwomba ciCopi,
 Edyani neŋgawomba ciSutu.

 Aŋga kaMalanje maniruketela miciwomba ciCopi,
 Edyani neŋgawomba ciSutu.

THE LYRICS: POETIC JUSTICE

*Unahoka kaMagule Katini inkuweta timbila
Mwama Nkulu vasinya kuwona waCopi.
MaΣaŋgana macipṣuala woku 'Ho-ho siyana'.
Wacipindwa ŋgukulosa Nkoma.
Aŋga kaMalanje maniruketela miciwomba ciCopi,
Edyani neŋgawomba ciSutu.*

Malanje says, 'You swear at me if you speak Chichopi,'
So I will speak Chisotho.

Malanje says, 'You swear at me if you speak Chichopi,'
So I will speak Chisotho.

Katini will come to Magule to play *Timbila*.
The President is glad to see the WaChopi.
The Shangaans are left to sing their 'Ho-ho siyana'
Until very late for the President.

Malanje says, 'You swear at me if you speak Chichopi,'
So I will speak Chisotho.

Malanje was a Sotho, foreman or 'boss boy' at one of the mines (I think the Rose Deep) where Katini had gone to work in Johannesburg. This man could not speak the language of the Chopi and complained that it sounded like swearing when they spoke to him in their own tongue. So most obligingly they learnt to speak Chisotho for his benefit. This line has no connexion with the other verse of the song, but I gathered from Katini that the flow of the words fascinated him and established his melody.

The four-line verse again refers to the outstanding event in the district for some years, the visit of President Carmona. There is no love lost between the Chopi and the Shangaans whom they rather look down on. The Shangaans had failed to conquer the Chopi in the days when they swept up through the country from Natal and established themselves on the right bank of the Limpopo. The Chopi maintain, with good reason, that Shangaan music is simple and monotonous. They always seem to sing the same words over and over again, *Ho-ho siyana*, and this fact is used as a gibe against them. Consequently, when the President came to Magule it was the brilliant musicianship of the Chopi which appeared to attract his attention, and it was not until very late in the day that the Shangaans were allowed to sing for him. In the meanwhile the Chopi had been in the front rows, leaving the Shangaans waiting their turn somewhat disconsolately in the background. This verse I noticed always raised a humorous smile on the Chopi faces, illustrating the poetic justice of the situation.

6th Movement. JIBUDU. The Second Dance

> Nzinda kaNyabindini uhumili Kapitini tiwomba Zavala
> Maŋganakana cimapfa acileŋga,
> Miciwona Kapitini utela cicaŋgo cakwe
> Cicaŋgo caNyabindini.

> To the village of Nyabindini came Kapitini, says Zavala.
> You men, keep it dark
> That you saw Kapitini coming to this woman,
> This woman of Nyabindini.

Kapitini is an elder, a chief's messenger, of the Zavala district whom Katini had occasion to dislike. His previous *Ŋgodo*, the 4th Movement, *Mdano*, gives an account of the incident which contributed to his dislike of the man. This piece of scandal about him must have been gladly seized upon by Katini to discomfort Kapitini, who seems to have been a somewhat officious character. The verse is clever, as Katini makes the statement of Kapitini's indiscretion appear to come from the Paramount Chief himself. His injunction to the young men to keep it dark, so dark that they sing it out at the top of their voices, must have been a delightful revenge when it was first performed in the new *Ŋgodo*. The sharp tongue of the poet-composer must be a weapon to be reckoned with by those in a Chopi village foolish enough to be found out. From what they tell me Katini's dislike of the man was generally shared, which would have made the song all the better.

7th Movement. MZENO. The Song

> Hiŋganyeŋgisa
> Masiŋgita
> Ciŋgolanini wadikona kufide Cindodani
> Kupwata nekuloŋga Cindodani we Cileni
> Kulondisa tate wakwe
> Hatikuni uciwapfa vacileŋga
> Kundaba yawukoma.

> Wani Zavale wakumusiya kadeya Manjeŋgwe
> Tate waŋgu kupwata ne salane
> Kupwata ne kusalane Zavala
> Atsula msaho ne Refiboa inawona mihumbo.

THE LYRICS: POETIC JUSTICE

Asinyisilwe timbila hagarini hokamati aluwanje
Iŋgandi citsuula mawhaiye
Acihuma ninkuluŋgwani
Devesiyane mwanana waNyabindini
Etsambisa timbila.

Mweno Manceŋgwe wafambelana usati kwia cica
Eraya damaduwa a Manjeŋgwe
Kainambi mona
Uciwomba nimakuhu maŋgwana niŋgakonwa
Utisa ne Cinzavane wa Manjeŋgwe
Sikati wa matuwa.[1]

Listen
To the mysteries!
At Chingolanini it is said there died Chindodani.
In poverty he died, this Chindodani of Chileni,
To follow his father.
We hear this death is hushed up.
It is an affair of the Chiefs.

Wani Zavala, you left Manjengwe in prison,
So he did not say 'good-bye' to you,
Not even say 'good-bye', Zavala,
When we went to play *Msaho* at Lisbon, there to see wonders.

We made new tunes for the *Timbila* in the midst of the sea
As we passed foreign lands.
She came warbling,
Dewesiyane daughter of Nyabindini,
To encourage the *Timbila*.

You, Manjengwe, why did you go and die?
Now you are dead, Manjengwe,
We shall not see you again.
If you appeared we should not believe our eyes.
Ask Chinzawane,
Ask Chinzawane, wife of Manjengwe,
About his death.

This song is a lament for the death of Katini's great friend Manjengwe. The two of them were fellow musicians and composers and held much the same relationship as David and Jonathan. Manjengwe was of royal blood, being the son of a previous Paramount Chief and in the line of succession for the chieftainship,

[1] Each verse is sung twice.

and Katini the commoner was his inseparable friend. Katini must have been the better musician of the two. He was always the orchestra leader as his father had been before him and as his gifted son is likely to be after him. Manjengwe played the *Saŋge*, alto xylophone, on Katini's left, the usual position in the orchestra for the second in command.

The circumstances surrounding his death were unfortunate. He went with Katini's orchestra, the *Ŋgodo* of Zavala, with their womenfolk to the Tercentenary Celebrations in Lisbon in 1940. They stayed there from June to September, demonstrating their music and dances in the exhibition grounds. Then Manjengwe caught a severe chill which turned to pneumonia, and he died. He was buried in Lisbon and his widow returned without him. To die away from home in a foreign country is always a distressing thought to Africans, and one can see how much this must have grieved Katini. But that was not all. There had been an estrangement between Manjengwe and his near relative, the present Paramount Chief. It was over some minor court case when the payment of a fine or a word on his behalf from Wani Zavala to the Magistrate might have released him from prison. But neither was forthcoming, and Manjengwe blamed Wani for his hard-heartedness and, in fact, implied that he had not helped him because he was a possible claimant to the chieftainship. This insinuation explains the reference to Chindodani.

The story of the death of Chindodani is one of intrigue amongst jealous relatives who wanted the chieftainship of Chileni to go to another. Chindodani also died away from his home at Chingolanini, under suspicious circumstances. It was freely said in those parts, they tell me, that his death was not unwelcome to certain elders who kept the fact of his father's demise a secret until they had got their own candidate for the position back from the Rand where he was working in the gold-mines. In other words, had Chindodani come into his chieftainship as the eldest son of Chileni the odds are that he would not have died in poverty but would have been alive still. Hence the reference to this affair, implying that the intrigues of the men in power were in both cases responsible for a certain amount of distress to innocent folk. There seems little doubt that Katini the poet and musician had hoped that some day his friend would become Paramount Chief, the next Zavala, and in some degree he held Wani Zavala to

THE LYRICS: POETIC JUSTICE

blame for Manjengwe's death, because of his unkindness to him before he went away to Lisbon to die in exile.

Naturally, when the *Ŋgodo* left for Lisbon, Manjengwe who still felt sore about the affair did not go to say good-bye to the Chief. It appears there is a custom that anyone leaving the territory should first go to the Chief, if not for his permission, at least for his blessing. The association in Katini's mind is clear on this point. The lack of the Chief's blessing must also have contributed, he thought, towards Manjengwe's death. When Katini came to Durban with me I noticed he made a point of saying good-bye to Wani Zavala. He had left it very late before the bus was due and I had discouraged him, as he might have failed to return in time from the village where Zavala was staying some two miles away. Luckily Zavala himself turned up at the village of Quissico from where we left and bade us all good-bye.

Katini says he composed several new tunes while on board ship between Lourenço Marques and Lisbon. The ship which took them over was a month on the journey and they skirted the coast in several places on the way, close enough for them to see the unfamiliar contours of many strange lands from a distance.

They took their womenfolk with them as they were to be away six months or so, and besides, the women were to help with the cooking and take a quiet part in the dancing. They do not dance with the men, but encourage them with warbling cries or ululations and do little shuffling *pas seuls* in front of the line of dancers when the spirit moves them. Dewesiyane, daughter of Nyabindini, they say, was rather a favourite with them and she danced and cheered them on better than any of the others. So Katini must needs mention this fact as part of the story of the last chapter of Manjengwe's life. The injunction in the last verse to ask Chinzawane his wife about his death is poignant in the extreme, conjuring up as it does the days of anxiety and distress she must have experienced as her man slipped away from her in this land of strangers.

The music for this *Mzeno* movement is one of Katini's best compositions, and is the musical climax of the *Ŋgodo*.

8th Movement. MABANDLA. *The Councillors*
Wani Zavale!
Kumaha kumusindo we Zavale,

Wuciwambo kumviso
Heti wakoma wadzawalini!

Timbila takutsamba takuusa usiwana necihuma miroŋgo,
Ticisikwa ŋguKatini timbila
Naŋgowamba necisinya.

Wani Zavale!
Kumaha kumusindo we Zavale,
Wuciwambo kumviso
Heti wakoma wadzawalini!

Wani Zavala!
Hush, you people of Zavala,
Cease your chatter
At this kraal of Chiefs!

Timbila music is so moving it brings tears,
This music of Katini's *Timbila*
Singing and dancing.

Wani Zavala!
Hush, you people of Zavala,
Cease your chatter,
At this kraal of Chiefs.

This poem of Katini's is in the familiar strain of the musician advertising himself and his music, and not without justification. His love of his music and the hold it has on the people are unquestioned. After all, if anyone is to sing the praises of his art, who else is there to do it except himself, the composer and poet of the village? Wani Zavala's name is again invoked, and you will have noticed that it can be pronounced in several ways, Zavala, Zavale, or Zavale. In the Mangeni district he is sometimes called Zaline. The singing of this poem ends the dance, which is performed by the dancers in two groups representing two rival bands of councillors. All through the dance they have been divided, but now at the end they join up again into one line to sing this poem.

9th Movement. NJIRIRI. The Dancers' Finale
Atuhakuwona!
Akudziwa mwanana wavakwanu wokunyisa wurindi.
Katini wakuwona acilaŋga.
Hambi cikudziwa walaŋgwa ŋguKatini musiki watimbila.
Atuhakudziwa!

THE LYRICS: POETIC JUSTICE

We see you!
We know you are leading that child astray.
Katini sees you but keeps quiet.
Although he knows it all right he keeps quiet, Katini, the leader of *Timbilas*.
We know you!

Early in 1943 Katini happened to find out that a member of his village was seducing a girl who was too young to be courted. So he took this means to put a stop to it. Imagine the shock to the guilty person who discovers he has been found out, and although not mentioned by name he must wonder how many know about it. He, as one of the dancers, might even be forced to sing it out loud with the rest of them, wondering all the time whether the others' laughter was against him and the predicament he was in, or whether it was not. In any case he would have to keep a straight face and sing it out.

Here we see the salutary effect of the village poet's use of his talents for a keenly moral and social end. It is most certainly a force to be reckoned with by transgressors against the codes of society. For as long as the song is in use as a part of the current *Ŋgodo*, a matter of a year or more, the far from silent warning will hang over his head.

3. ŊGODO

Composed in 1940 by Gomukomu, orchestral leader and composer, at the village of Chief Filippe Banguza, Zavala District

MOVEMENTS

1. *Msitso wokata.*   The First Orchestral Introduction.
2. *Msitso wombidi.*   The Second Orchestral Introduction.
3. *Msitso woraru.*   The Third Orchestral Introduction.
4. *Ŋgeniso.*   The Entry of the Dancers.
5. *Mdano.*   The Call of the Dancers.
6. *Cidanuwana Combidi.*   The Second Call of the Dancers.
7. *Cibudo.*   The Dance.
8. *Mzeno.*   The Song.
9. *Mabandla.*   The Councillors.
10. *Njiriri Cive kwako Ŋgoma.*   Dancers' Finale with Drums.
11. *Msitso kugwita.*   Orchestral Finale.

Movements 1, 2, and 3 are all introductions without words as the dancers have not yet appeared on the dance floor in front of the orchestra. It will be noticed that at this village the word is *Msitso* and not *Musitso* as it is in the eastern part of the Zavala district. The people of Banguza maintain that this is better ChiChopi.

4th Movement. ŊGENISO. *The Entry of the Dancers*

    Dhlalani maŋgoma!
    Dhlalani wakoma vanizonda!
    Dhlalani maŋgoma![1]

    Hear, you diviners!
    Hear, the dead are against me!
    Hear, you diviners!

The injunction to the diviners needs little explanation to any African, but it is not so easy to find a direct European equivalent to-day; not that we do not call upon the unseen powers but that our symbols have changed. Who has not felt at one time or another when luck was dead out that even 'the dead are against you'? 'Luck' is perhaps the nearest equivalent.

5th Movement. MDANO. *The Call of the Dancers*

Hawula njowu!
Uwalu jovelu maΣaŋgana udyiwa ŋguvaSutu.

Hawula njowu!
Uwalu jovelu maΣaŋgana udyiwa ŋguvaSutu.
Udyiwa ŋguvaSutu nimaXosa hakwambi uziva.

Udyiwa ŋguvaSutu nimaXosa hakwambi uziva.

Vehoka kajimu hasanguni inkufela ukoma.
Vehoka kajimu hasanguni inkufela ukoma
Hambiza wakuku kicini ndani vatiziwa.

Hambiza wakuku kicini ndani vatiziwa.

Hawula njowu!
Uwalu jovelu maΣaŋgana udyiwa ŋguvaSutu.

Cast off your skins!
There is no relish left, you Shangaans, it has been eaten by the Sotho.
Cast off your skins!
There is no relish left, you Shangaans, it has been eaten by the Sotho.
It has been eaten by the Sotho and the Xhosa, and we will not get it.
It has been eaten by the Sotho and the Xhosa, and we will not get it.

      [1] Verse repeated three times.

THE LYRICS: POETIC JUSTICE

They came to the gatekeeper and wanted good jobs.
They came to the gatekeeper and wanted good jobs.
Even the cooks in the kitchen know it.
Even the cooks in the kitchen know it.
Cast off your skins!
There is no relish left, you Shangaans, it has been eaten by the Sotho.

The setting is one of the Rand gold-mines. The Shangaans and the Chopi have come up from Portuguese East Africa recruited for work on the mines. They are foreigners in South Africa and the other tribes make them remember it. It seems to be a well-known custom, they say, to bribe the native police guard at the compound gate to speak on their behalf to the compound manager in order to get them good jobs. The bribe is never refused, but the good jobs are as few and far between as ever. Since the gatekeepers are usually local natives, what pickings there are go to their own people, the Sotho and Xhosa tribesmen. The Zulus are not mentioned because they dislike work on the mines and constitute an insignificant proportion of the total of mine workers.

'Cast off your skins', like the 'Rend your garments' of the Old Testament, is an expression of sorrow and anger, of resignation to defeat and shame. It refers to the skin aprons commonly worn in the country. There is little doubt, from what compound managers tell me, that this kind of bribery is common and it must be irksome to those who fall for it unsuccessfully. The life of the mine labourer is now the usual experience of a large proportion of able-bodied Chopi. It is not surprising to find so much mention of it in their songs.

6th Movement. CIDANUWANA COMBIDI. The Second Call of the Dancers

Hawiyeza vakuyadinda zulu!
Lavanani nivakatanu micaŋga tapfa mdano.
Hawiyeza vakuyadinda zulu!
Lavanani nivakatanu micaŋga tapfa mdano.
Kusika timbila ŋgumaha ŋgu ndoro vaMaŋgeni vahihluti
Kusika timbila ŋgumaha ŋgu ndoro vaMaŋgeni vahihluti
Mihumbo yamina Ŋguyusa majaha,
Mihumbo kuteka tipondo tamina amanu nisava nzila.

Mihumbo yamina Ŋguyusa majaha,
Mihumbo kuteka tipondo tamina amanu nisava nzila.
Wasihora nana bombele yasona sotembisa sibayani.
Wasihora nana bombele yasona sotembisa sibayani
Watembo wuuŋgwadla niusiwana wacibayani cahambanza.
Watembo wuuŋgwadla niusiwana wacibayani cahambanza.
Hawiyeza vakuyadinda zulu!
Lavanani nivakatanu micaŋga tapfa mdano.

Hark how the music thunders!
Listen with your wives and hear the Call.
Hark how the music thunders!
Listen with your wives and hear the Call.
To play the *Timbila* you must dream about it so that we of Mangeni will excel in it.
To play the *Timbila* you must dream about it so that we of Mangeni will excel in it.
This wonder of mine, my young brother Nguyusa,
This wonder—to take my money to buy the right of way!
This wonder of mine, my young brother Nguyusa,
This wonder—to take my money to buy the right of way!
You girls, you adorn yourselves with marks to attract us.
You girls, you adorn yourselves with marks to attract us,
With these marks you attract us on forehead and temples.
With these marks you attract us on forehead and temples.
Hark how the music thunders!
Listen with your wives and hear the Call.

This lyric is in the grand tradition of the minstrels whose hearts are wrapped up in their art. Their genuine love of their music is patent to anyone who gets to know them intimately. They are never far from their instruments, they practise for hours, they compose new variations, and they are always eager for an excuse to play with full orchestra and dancers. The intense percussive thrill of a full *Timbila* orchestra of twenty or more players is an experience never to be forgotten. But it is not all noise, it is an intricate weaving of patterns both on the instruments and by the dancers, in well-directed shapes and forms. There is not a shadow of the dilettante about them; here are music and poetry as they should be. So when they sing 'Hark how the music thunders' they mean just that. The music trills and reverberates through the trees in a concord of sound which only great orchestras can give.

The Call is the *Mdano* movement when the dancers perform their second dance and sing their 'Call'.

It is no exaggeration to say that to play the *Timbila* well you must dream about it. The dexterity of the good player is a delight to watch, and Gomukomu, the composer of this poem and music, has the reputation of being the most gifted exponent of them all.

The various villages are proud of their musicians and dancers and they strive to excel in their performances. They hold competitions (*Msaho*) in which the orchestras compete against each other. The musicians of the Mangeni district, under their Chief, Filippe Banguza, were specially recommended to me and they lived up to their reputation. In Durban, European musicians were particularly impressed by the sheer musicianship they displayed in all their work.

'This wonder of mine . . . to take my money to buy the right of way' will seem strange to us who are so used to transport of all kinds. It refers to the coming of motor-cars and railways into their country. Before they came everyone walked, a journey was your own journey on your own flat feet, every inch of it by your own effort, and you walked where you pleased. Now they offered you a journey sitting in a vehicle over your own country and took your money for it! How marvellous! To buy the road, the journey, without effort! How remarkable!

There is a story told about the Zulu of Natal in the early days when the railway was first opened along the coast of Zululand. They crowded down to the station to see the train and to take a ride to Durban. But when they heard they had to pay for a ticket before they could get on the train they replied 'Not on your life! What! pay for travelling across your own country?— No Nkosi! The train is only going to the same place as we are going. We'll get there in our own time.' So these instinctive socialists proudly walked off along the well-worn foot-paths, their ancestral right of way.

The marks Gomukomu refers to are the cicatrices with which the young girls adorn themselves, patterns cut into the skin, a custom commonly practised by many Bantu people. Chopi marks are great weals and lumps, like the hide of a crocodile, the very antithesis of our idea of beauty. There is, they say, a movement amongst the younger generation to drop the custom of cutting their bodies, but the marks on the forehead and temples still persist.

7th Movement. CIBUDO. The Dance

    Lavanani maŋganakana kuvusha mbaŋgo wakuhlula nimaGeremani.
    Lavanani maŋganakana kuvusha mbaŋgo wakuhlula nimaGeremani.
    O—o, ŋgotawona Igodo!

    Come along, you men, and join up to fight the Germans.
    Come along, you men, and join up to fight the Germans.
    Oh—ho, Come and hear the Show!

Although the colony of Moçambique was neutral in the war, the close association of the Chopi with the Rand mines in South Africa leads them towards a certain association of thought with the events in that country. This poem, composed at the beginning of the war about 1940, naturally reflects the feeling of the times. The last line has a ring of 'Come on and hear, Alexander's Rag Time Band', as if what really mattered to them was the Show, and let the world go by.

8th Movement. MZENO. The Song

Lavanani micaŋga sika timbila tamakono.
Howotawa ditsimbirini kavaluŋgu.
Ŋguyusa mwana atu kunevuneti timbila tamakono.
Nopwata Mzeno uuwa timbila.
A-koŋga ko nimafuiye Gomukomu watu.
A-koŋga ko nimafuiye Gomukomu watu,
Kwalakanya nyumbani kamina ko nopemberuka noka.
Maninya Mtumbu vasumako kutsura nikubilivila.
Maninya Mtumbu vasumako kutsura nikubilivila.
Mane woruwala cibembe ciya cawulombe.
Dabwa Lakeni wadanwa ŋkoma.
Filipe, mwana atu, unagwita unkudava ŋgwaluŋgu.
Awi Lakeni, wakuruma ako mahuŋgu akutala.
Awi Lakeni, wakuruma ako mahuŋgu akutala
O upsala kudoŋgola nesiŋgaŋgo.
UaZandameleni madanwa mahuŋgu.
Ŋgoŋgondo utavile mahuŋgu ŋgundawa yakusela.
Lavanani micaŋga sika timbila tamakono.[1]

[1] Each verse is repeated twice with the exception of the last line.

PLATE III

a. Gomukomu with his *saŋge timbila*

b. The village *timbila* orchestra

PLATE IV

The *Ŋgodo* of musicians and dancers at Mavila's village resting in the shade while I took down the poetry and they repeated each movement without the dances. The man on the right is sitting on a *Nvinga* drum

Come together and make music for the new year!
We fear only that our names will be written by the white men.
Nguyusa, my young brother, help me compose my music.
I have no 'Great Song' for my *Timbila*.
You said you would care for me, my Gomukomu,
You said you would care for me, my Gomukomu,
But now in my house I am left weaving alone.
Maninya Mtumbu, you think you are beautiful because you are fair!
Maninya Mtumbu, you think you are beautiful because you are fair!
But you surely are sweet as the bees!
Lakeni the messenger has come to call you.
Filippe, our 'child', they will be the death of you with their calling.
You, Lakeni, are sent on important affairs.
You, Lakeni, are sent on important affairs,
Yet you dally on the road, joking with the girls.
You people of Zandamela are called to the Court.
Ngongondo, you fear the Court on account of your drinking.
Come together and make music for the new year!

Gomukomu, as we said, is one of the best musicians in the country of the Chopi. His musical idiom is mature and compelling. The orchestral setting of this *Mzeno*, or Great Song, is one of his best works with a strong melodic outline and full orchestral ground. The change of mood in the third verse of the poem is moving and the whole composition shows the hand of a master. Yet he does not hesitate to recognize the element of community composition which the rest of his orchestra brings to the work. So we get the impression of a concerted effort of all the musicians to make a grand job of the *Mzeno*, which always seems to be the highlight of a *Ŋgodo*. Here they are in the shade of their *mukusu* trees learning to fit in their parts to his new composition for the coming year's orchestral dances.

'We fear only that our names will be written.' This means that they hope their names will not be put down for work outside the district, either on the sugar estates or the banana plantations of the Inkomati valley, or on the Rand mines, for that would deprive them of the pleasures of taking part in the new year's *Ŋgodo*. Gomukomu openly states that he dislikes the idea of leaving home at any time if he has to forgo his music and so tries to avoid having his name put down.

Nguyusa, his younger brother, is also a composer and poet and so is his second brother Mahlabezulu, who once recorded for H.M.V. in Johannesburg. The record he made then bears his name. Their father before them was the orchestra leader of their village and all three have inherited the father's gift. The pity of it is that we have no records of the music of past generations.

The third verse is supposed to be the words of Gomukomu's young wife, who finds her musician husband rather trying and wedded to his music. She sits at home doing this and that, weaving to and fro, as an animal weaves in a cage, waiting for her husband to come home from his *Timbila* playing.

Maninya Mtumbo is a young beauty of the village. She has fair skin which is considered an asset amongst the Chopi, and although she is proud of it, Gomukomu grants her the compliment of being as sweet as the bees—not 'as honey' as we would say, but still a 'honey'.

Lakeni is a messenger employed by the Administrador at his office to take messages to the Mangeni district. Each district has its own messenger, I understand. Lakeni does not happen to be popular. It is after all a job in which it is possible to put on airs or to take small advantages. So the face of Lakeni round the door is not always a good sign. Filippe Banguza may have to go off again the thirty or so long miles through the sandy bush country to the office to fix up another of those cases with the Administrador. They are fairly frequent, and as yet he has no easy means of transport to the office. He has the heart-felt sympathies of his villagers who know what a bother it is to go all that way; 'They will be the death of him with their calling!' In any case, they don't like that fellow Lakeni, especially when he has an important message and loiters around with the girls on the way. And talking of Lakeni the messenger, reminds him of the people of the next village who all got into trouble recently. Zandamela, they say, was once the best village in the whole Zavala district with a great personality, Mahlatini, as their Chief. His son, Ngongondo, has not kept up the reputation of his father and drink has been at the bottom of it. It is quite remarkable, even to a visitor, how much the people of a village reflect the character of their Chief. The people of Banguza and their neighbours of Zandamela provide a clear example of the two opposites.

Leadership in Chopi villages still means a great deal to the happiness of the villagers.[1]

9th Movement. MABANDLA. The Councillors
Kuwatiswa timbila taMaŋgeni takupwata niinceka
Filipe kuniwone kuhlupeka nepwata nibaci.

Kuwatiswa timbila taMaŋgeni takupwata niinceka
Filipe kuniwone kuhlupeka nepwata nibaci.

Vavasikati kuminevuni hicaŋgadila Kaleci
Mfana waBaleka, Kaleci, wakudawa yguwukoma.

I made *Timbila* for Mangeni, yet I have no clothes.
Filippe, can you not see I am distressed without even a coat!
I made *Timbila* for Mangeni, yet I have no clothes.
Filippe, can you not see I am distressed without even a coat!
You women, help us to lament Kalechi.
This son of Baleka, Kalechi, he died because he was an only son and heir.

It will be immediately clear that this poem is not from the same brain. It is in fact the song of an older musician of the mendicant type, father of Majanyana, the present instrument-maker. The craft of making xylophones, the *Timbila*, runs in families, and there is a certain pride in this fact. Majanyana, the son, is now the official instrument-maker to Mangeni, that is, to the present holder of the title, Chief Filippe Banguza. His old father died in 1939 or thereabouts, and in memory of him Gomukomu put one of his songs into his new 1940 *Ŋgodo*. It is the pleasant tribute of one musician to another, and an example of the recognition of a kind of guild of craftsmen which Chopi musicians seem to have.

The mendicant musician is more common in Rhodesia, where the name *Rombe* means a 'travelling musician'. They are not of the social status of our street singers, outcasts and objects of pity, but rather of the wandering minstrel or bard, who in our history would stroll from castle to castle and from village to village entertaining the people and making a precarious living in that way. There do not seem to be many wandering players amongst the Chopi. The high incidence of orchestras in nearly every large village and their fixed establishment would undermine

[1] For further analysis of this movement see Appendix IV.

the demand for wandering minstrels unless they had something very special to offer.

The people of Mangeni were very sorry at the death of Kalechi, who was a comparatively young man when he died, and popular. He was an only son and heir to the chieftainship of his father Baleka, a lesser chief or *induna* of that district. It was just his luck, they thought, to have to lose his only son. Had he had a large family, nine chances out of ten it would not have happened. The question of inheritance and of having a son or daughter to perpetuate their line is of the greatest importance to African families and is constantly behind the words of their songs.

The name Kalechi is a sign of the modern times. A large proportion of Chopi natives to-day have English names. Many have Portuguese names too, such as Zhuwau (Portuguese, João), but the fashion seems to be towards English names. It comes perhaps from their close association with the Rand mines. This name Kalechi is, of course, the English word 'carriage', but I do not attempt to give the correct foreign spelling, for in any case the pronunciation is already indigenous, and a long way from the original.

10th Movement. NJIRIRI CIUE KWAKO ŊGOMA

This movement is accompanied by drums, two drums, the *Ŋgoma*, a large one, and *Nzoma*, a small one. Between them they kick up such a noise that singing is quite out of the question. In fact the playing of drums with the orchestra is not popular in some villages. I asked a group of representative musicians why this was, and they said that only two villages now retained the custom, Banguza and Nyakutowo; the rest of them preferred to hear the music of the *Timbila*. I can sympathize with them, for the drums certainly engulfed the music, but, on the other hand, the playing of the drums for just one or two of the movements, usually the Entry and the Exit of the Dancers, adds a touch of excitement and variety which we could appreciate. Perhaps a compromise in which the drums took their part but not prominently during the singing would be the best answer. It would be a pity if the custom died out altogether.

It is amusing to see the performers on the drums. The larger drum *Ŋgoma* is played with two wooden beaters with heavy heads. But the smaller is played with light sticks very rapidly and is held by a little boy over his shoulder. The drummer stands or kneels behind him and, it appears, miraculously avoids whipping the little boy's ear off.

11th Movement. MSITSO KUGWITA. Orchestral Finale

Like other orchestral finales, this has no poem and is the repeat of the first orchestral introduction.

This completed Gomukomu's 1940 *Ŋgodo*, a work full of character and musical skill. It was the second *Ŋgodo* he had completed as leader of the *Igodo* at Banguza's kraal. It is now no longer performed and has been replaced by his 1942/3 *Ŋgodo*. By the end of 1943 he was already working on his fourth *Ŋgodo* which was to be performed in 1944.

4. ŊGODO

Composed in 1942/3 by Gomukomu, orchestral leader and composer at the village of Chief Filippe Banguza, Zavala District

MOVEMENTS

1. *Msitso wokata.*   First Orchestral Introduction.
   Msitso wombidi.   Second Orchestral Introduction.
   Msitso woraru.   Third Orchestral Introduction.
   Msitso womune.   Fourth Orchestral Introduction.
   Msitso woklanu.   Fifth Orchestral Introduction.
2. *Ŋgeniso.*   The Entry of the Dancers.
3. *Ndano.*   The Call of the Dancers.
4. *Cidana cacidoko.*   The Little Call.
5. *Cibudo coosinye.*   The Dance.
6. *Cibudo coosinye kambe.*   The Second Dance.
7. *Mzeno.*   The Song.
8. *Nsumeto Mabandla.*   Preparation for the Councillors.
9. *Mabandla.*   The Councillors.
10. *Yokugwitisa yeŋgoma.*   The Drum Finale.
11. *Msitso wokata kugumiro.*   The Orchestral Finale.

1st Movement. MSITSO, in five parts

This *Ŋgodo* is remarkable in that Gomukomu has composed no less than five orchestral introductions. None of them has words upon which to base its theme and they are all works of original musicality. They demonstrate in no uncertain manner the reputation Gomukomu possesses as a composer.

2nd Movement. ŊGENISO. *The Entry of the Dancers (with Drums)*

    Suŋgeta ŋguwo-o-o-o-o-o!
    O we-e-e-e,
    Suŋgeta ŋguwo!

    Gird up your loins-o-o-o-o-o!
    O we-e-e-e,
    Gird up your loins!

The words of this movement are very brief because the music is accompanied by the two drums *Ŋgoma* and *Nzoma* which would drown any ordinary song.

It is just an injunction to the dancers to hitch up their loin-cloths as they come in, in preparation for the dance. The dance in the 4th and 5th Movements is so energetic that the injunction is certainly not misplaced.

3rd Movement. NDANO. *The Call of the Dancers*

Mahuŋgwa a Filipe
Akuna bala ndwendwe wasihora nana.
Mahuŋgwa a Filipe
Akuna bala ndwendwe wasihora nana
Mahuŋgwa a Filipe
Akutsamba kuwia nendwendwe!

Gomukomu mwana atu,
Uani votisile vacikona mwaya ŋguwatu herande.
Gomukomu mwana atu,
Uani votisile vacikona mwaya ŋguwatu herande
Guwotiswa ŋguwakoma!

Eyo waŋgani dayela Makomo
Wo homane nowusiku amanu ecipeka nyiwo.
Eyo waŋgani dayela Makomo
Wo homane nowuisku amanu ecipeka nyiwo
Unawona katavane acanawela unagwita inkudawa.

Awe Lakeni woteka nemakanju ucatsimbisa.
Unagwita inkukudaya.
Awe Lakeni woteka nemakanju ucatsimbisa
Unagwita inkukudaya.

Awe Lakeni, ntimaŋgade lahle
Mwana Nyamandane watisa.
Awe Lakeni, ntimaŋgade lahle
Mwana Nyamandane watisa.

Mahuŋgwa a Filipe
Akuna bala ndwendwe wasihora nana.
Mahuŋgwa a Filipe
Akuna bala ndwendwe wasihora nana
Mahuŋgwa a Filipe
Akutsamba kuwia nendwendwe!

It is Filippe's opinion
That the girls also should sign on and go to the mines.
It is Filippe's opinion
That the girls also should sign on and go to the mines.
It is Filippe's opinion.
What a good idea!
Gomukomu our beloved,
No kraal is a good kraal unless it's full of women; take your choice.
Gomukomu our beloved,
No kraal is a good kraal unless it's full of women; take your choice.
Even Chiefs' daughters say so!
The one who killed Makomo
Will go out and weep in the night.
The one who killed Makomo
Will go out and weep in the night.
He may even take another man's wife and so meet his death.
You Lakeni, you refuse us the Cazhu fruit.
You will be the death of us!
You Lakeni, you refuse us the Cazhu fruit.
You will be the death of us!
You Lakeni, you are as black as coal,
Son of Nyamandane, you are a terror!
You Lakeni, you are as black as coal,
Son of Nyamandane, you are a terror!
It is Filippe's opinion
That the girls also should sign on and go to the mines.
It is Filippe's opinion
That the girls also should sign on and go to the mines.
It is Filippe's opinion.
What a good idea!

You can just see the harassed face of the Chief, Filippe Banguza, surrounded by a mass of emotional young women with all their menfolk away working on the Rand mines. No wonder it is his opinion that it would be a good thing if only they would sign on too and go to the mines with their husbands and their lovers. 'And so say all of us', echo the young men, 'Why not?' In this simple statement lies one of the major social problems of all the areas from which the Rand mines draw their labourers.

Gomukomu, the composer of this song, is not unaware that his looks and talents attract a certain amount of attention. Anyway, he is not above making himself out to be rather a lad although once happily married already; but polygamy has its points—even chiefs' daughters know that, and they are jealous enough and hard to please, heaven knows.

Makomo is the name of Gomukomu's grandfather. He was the *Musiki waTimbila*, the leader of the orchestra in his time, and his time, they believed, had been cut short. Why should he have had such pains in his belly and died so suddenly? Who was at the bottom of this? Whoever it was, he had not been found; but let his bones rot for causing the death of so fine a man and musician as Makomo. 'Let him go out and weep in the night; let him be caught in adultery and come to a bad end!' There were suspicions in a certain direction and, if they were true, that should make him squirm.

In 1940 Gomukomu had had occasion to lampoon Lakeni the messenger in his *Mzeno* for that year—that fellow Lakeni, the messenger, who put on airs and dallied with the girls when he should be about his business. Now, if you please, Lakeni had refused to allow his neighbours to make cider from the fruit of the Cazhu nut trees in his fields and near his hut. He did not need them; he was not living at home anyway; he was always at the office unless he was sent on a message. He is dark skinned, too, like his nature, black as coal! What a mean blighter, what a terror!

All the same, Filippe's idea is a good one, don't you think?

4th Movement. CIDANA CACIDOKO. The Little Call

Lavanani micitengisa
Lavanani newakatano micitabva Ndano.

Lavanani micitengisa
Lavanani newakatano micitabva Ndano.
Njane timbila mikone tsimba kusika takanane kwangu?

Njane timbila mikone tsimba kusika takanane kwangu?

THE LYRICS: POETIC JUSTICE

Ha! Wieza ſeŋgetile ſibando ſaka ſeŋgetile
Ciŋgolela camaboi.
Ha! Wieza ſeŋgetile ſibando ſaka ſeŋgetile
Ciŋgolela camaboi.
Natanele konevune ciluŋgu utzumbelako ugukule.
Natanele konevune ciluŋgu utzumbelako ugukule.
Maŋganakana ambane mahuŋgo
Awu vamombako valuŋgu, tate wakwe kafuma.
Maŋganakana ambane mahuŋgo
Awu vamombako valuŋgu, tate wakwe kafuma.
Mafu kavabaŋgane waCopi malalane nimilaya!
Mafu kavabaŋgane waCopi malalane nimilaya!
Dikombo daKawane waŋgu cisihate
Mwanana wandoko acimaha noni mwananeyo waŋgu.
Dikombo daKawane waŋgu cisihate
Mwanana wandoko acimaha noni mwananeyo waŋgu.
Woteka nimasembe acatsivela ukoma wapinda.
Woteka nimasemba acatsivela ukoma wapinda.
Lavanani miciteŋgisa
Lavanani newakatano micitabva Ndano.

Come together and hear,
Come together with your wives and listen to Ndano.
Come together and hear,
Come together with your wives and listen to Ndano.
Don't you want the new *Timbila* music I make from my heart?
Don't you want the new *Timbila* music I make from my heart?
Ha! We quarrel again! The same old trouble.
The older girls must pay taxes.
Ha! We quarrel again! The same old trouble.
The older girls must pay taxes.
Natanele speak for me to the white man to let me be.
Natanele speak for me to the white man to let me be.
You elders must discuss affairs.
The one whom the white men appointed was the son of a commoner.
You elders must discuss affairs.
The one whom the white men appointed was the son of a commoner.
The Chopi no longer have right to their own country, let me tell you.
The Chopi no longer have right to their own country, let me tell you.

The sorrow of my Kawane, the mystery
Why your children all die, yet you are still young.
The sorrow of my Kawane, the mystery
Why your children all die, yet you are still young.
Now you cease to bear and take the inheritance of your dead children.
Now you cease to bear and take the inheritance of your dead children.
Come together and hear,
Come together with your wives and listen to Ndano.

The invitation to come along and join in the 'fun and games', to come and see the dancing and hear the music of the *Ŋgodo*, is a very frequently repeated line with Chopi musicians. It is certainly very good fun to all concerned and none the worse for a little advertising, particularly if you want to come along and hear the latest compositions of so gifted a composer as Gomukomu, which he says he makes from his 'heart'. In point of fact the seat of musical inspiration he indicated as his chest in the region of his diaphragm, an opinion which many musicians other than Africans would agree with, in spite of our more customary emphasis upon that poetically over-worked organ the heart.

'The same old trouble' they tell me has to do with the much-argued question as to whether unmarried women should be liable to pay taxes or not. Some hold that women over thirty or so who have not assumed their primary role in matrimony should share equal taxation and equal liberties with other bachelors. What backing there is for such an argument in official quarters I was not able to find out, or whether in fact bachelor girls were ever taxed.

The next line is a plea by Gomukomu to a friend of his, Natanele, who worked with the agency recruiting labour for the mines, to avoid bringing up his name as a possible labourer. He did not wish to have to go off to the mines and would much prefer to devote himself to his music. It would certainly be unfortunate if he ever had to do so, as original artists of his calibre are few and far between.

The next verse refers to an affair in local politics in which the Administrador of the district had to intervene and appoint a new chief, not of the royal house, but of another family. I am not certain which appointment is referred to in this case, but I rather think it is the same as that spoken of by Katini in his 1940 *Ŋgodo*, 8th Movement, *Mzeno*. The Bantu are very loyal to their royal houses and will put up with a great deal of inefficiency and even tyranny from their chiefs provided they are in the true line of descent. This is not surprising in a race which is for the most part 'Ancestor revering' if not 'Ancestor worshipping'. In this instance the Administrador had chosen a man who was obviously more fitted for the job both by force of character and ability. Nevertheless the common people, uninterested in small matters such as human progress and development, would have preferred to have the old reprobate of the royal house over them. The Administrador's lot, like that of Gilbert and Sullivan's policeman, is not always a happy one; and I know that, while doing the obviously right thing by our standards in appointing the stronger man to the position of chief, he had a sympathetic feeling for the opposition who expressed themselves through Gomukomu's mouth as not having a right to their own country any longer. It is a moot point with which European administrative officers must inevitably be faced again and again. Gomukomu himself gives the answer—it is the elders themselves who must take greater responsibility for the community.

His fourth verse is poignant with the sorrows of one who is denied the joy of living progeny. Kawane, Gomukomu's sister, is one of the wives of the Chief Filippe Banguza. She has had several children, some stillborn and the others living only for a few short days or weeks. Her grief has been shared by all her friends and relatives, and now she has decided to give up all hope of having a child alive. So they say she must content herself with the inheritance, the knowledge of what might have been had her children survived. She will be credited in the hereafter with the creation of all those small frail souls who could not come to their maturity, and so she will be comforted. A similar concept exists in Rhodesia where they say the spirits of children who die young go to a kind of spirit nursery where they are looked after by the old women ancestors of the tribe, there to enjoy a heavenly life for a certain span until in good time they return again to the great nucleus of the tribal past when finally all memory of them has become submerged in the wave of time.

In this one poem we get a vivid account of what was passing through Gomukomu's mind when he sat down to express in words and music the theme for the fourth movement of his new ballet.

5th Movement. CIBUDO COOSINYE. *The Dance*

    Nizambwa nyekile
    Nizambwa nyekile gumwana waŋgu adi ciluŋguni.
    Acinitona neciŋgwalaŋgwanda ninya tumbwane nintona
    Niŋguwo yantima.

    I am most distressed,
    I am most distressed as my man has gone off to work,
    And he does not give me clothes to wear,
    Not even black cloth.

Here we see the shadow of the mineshaft headgear thrown across the Limpopo river four hundred miles away and disrupting the family life of thousands of Africans. Her man is away and until he returns she can have little contact with him except by an occasional letter, scrawled perhaps in rickety handwriting by some friend of his, and after many weeks of uncertain postage read to her by some other friend. But perhaps no money will come until he does return, and in the meanwhile she has not even the cheapest cloth to clothe herself, not even that thin black stuff she might get from the Indian stores. It is hard, very hard on a girl, especially when those other girls have just bought themselves such nice clothes since their men came back a few weeks ago. The mines have entered into the souls of these people with the pangs of parting and constant separation.

6th Movement. CIBUDO COOSINYE KAMBE. *The Second Dance*

    Lavanani mootse miciteŋgisa tafaneyo Faife.
    Lavanani mootse miciteŋgisa tafaneyo Faife.

    Come, all of you and listen to the boy Faife.
    Come, all of you and listen to the boy Faife.

No need to waste a good poem on this movement. By the time the dancers got to the point where they ought to sing the lyric, they would be so exhausted with dancing those two most athletic movements that they would be out of breath. So let's content ourselves with this single line, which is quite good enough to hang a very good dancing melody on.

The boy Faife is the nephew of Gomukomu, son of Mahlabezulu. He is a bright lad who took to the *Timbila* as all good Chopi musicians should do at the age of about six or seven. Now

THE LYRICS: POETIC JUSTICE

at the age of twelve or so he is showing great promise of keeping up the family reputation for music, and is playing his instrument with great dexterity for a lad of his age. His name is just another example of the 'English' tradition, it is 'Five'.

7th Movement. MZENO. The Song
Hiŋgane malala necimigela kupguela kuhanya yeti mbaŋgo wamageremani.
Mahuŋgo aTsewane opwata nemwanana.

Waho wakwambe pekwa mpama guwakwawe.
Matijawo katilawe.
Bladifulu waluŋgu wacilwa
Fo nyawu ŋguni ruketela Matijawo.

Kwalakanye Ŋguyusa mwana atu kwasika timbila
Kanena mbaşa yasika timbila takutsamba
Timbila tona tisiya nicama famba.

Maho mamwane mabala solane awa vasikati wakuteka mbewu vaci fawa sopa.
Ŋguteka mbewu aciniŋgela kusela
Hiŋgeŋgisela O!
Magarafu maguuma!

Gutsiwelwa nzila guwakoma waZaline nevaNyabindini hicacisekweni.
Filipe mwana atu hedawisile Ŋguŋgundwane.
Awo Manjeŋgwe hinaŋgo hayi makono kaCamusi?
Dawoti nene acihikomba ŋguCikome.

Kupekwa manzane niwakoma wantumanini hiŋgeŋgisela
Dizaŋga daJulai mweno kupeka manzani
Kahena mbaşa hicambala mabuluku.
Kwalakanya Julai ŋgufuma acinawaluta dibuku.
Julai akoveŋgela niwa wasikati.

Ukwela citimela newakoma hiŋgahoka Sewe hicawomba wombe
Ŋgundawa yakuldya vacihitsuralela
Hicama mana maPortugezi mamba mahoŋgu ŋgudawa yakuldya
Ŋgundawa yakuldya vacihitsuralela.

Hiŋgane malala necimigela kupguela kuhanya yeti mbaŋgo wamageremani.
Mahuŋgo aTsewane opwata nemwanana.

Be quiet while we older people explain to you about the German war.
It is because Tsewane has no children.

Who would allow himself to be smacked in the face?
Matijawo wouldn't allow it.
The bloody fools of white men are fighting.
Matijawo says they are like four-legged beasts.

Think about playing *Timbila*, Nguyusa, my lad,
Because I am not composing any new music for the *Timbila* just now.
I will have to leave my *Timbila* behind when I go to the farm.
There are women foolish enough to take grain from the bins to sell for beer!
To take corn and waste it on drink...!
Listen, oh...?
... The bottle is empty!
The way to the court is closed by the Chiefs, by the people of Zavala and Nyabindini.
Filippe, our child, Ngungundwane troubles us with his constant calling.
And you, Manjengwe, how shall we go to Chamusi?
Dawoti says we must go by way of Chikome.
Even Chiefs are beaten on the hands, you people of Wantuma, listen.
The arrogance of Julai in even beating the hands of Chiefs!
We will not wear trousers any more.
Julai imagines he has opened a book.
Julai spares not even women.
We got on the train and arrived at Sewe,
And when we spoke about the matter of food,
About the matter of food, they turned their backs.
We overheard the Portuguese speaking about food,
Speaking about food while their backs were turned.
Be quiet while we older people explain to you about the German war.
It is because Tsewane has no children.

Here is another typical *Mzeno*, full of chatter, humour, and local gossip. It is particularly humorous, this number, and starts well by mockingly calling the people to hear some serious piece of information, only to find that the real, deep, underlying reason for this great war between the English and the Germans is because they are fighting over the local belle of the village, Tsewane. Tsewane, they say, is a noted courtesan over whom there has been a lot of hard and bitter rivalry among the young men of the district. They will be only too quick to appreciate the seriousness of the conflict between the English and the Germans in this light. In any case, who would allow himself to be smacked in the face? Matijawo, that hefty young six-footer, would not. Matijawo is a great lad at dancing, in fact the girls come specially to watch him dance, and he does everything else he takes up equally well, with that sly smile of his—the handsome blighter! He does not often have to fight with his weight and size, so that's why he says the bloody fools of white men are fighting like four-legged beasts—what the hell!

It seems clear that Gomukomu is out of cash again and he'll have to take the least painful way out—go to the banana plantations along the Inkomati river. He won't be able to take his *Timbila* with him and for several long months he will be bereft of his beloved music. But the banana plantations are the best employers in these parts: they look after you well, and you get good food, and besides you can get short-term contracts and hop on the 'Thornycroft' and be back in a day. All the same, as leader of the *Timbila* Orchestra he will have to leave someone to carry on his duties and lead the orchestra on Sunday afternoons; Sundays are his regular dance days when all the folk turn up. The other days are just by-days, playing for the fun of it. Now that Mahlabezulu, the second brother, is on a spell up at the mines it only leaves Nguyusa, the youngest brother, to keep the orchestra up to scratch. Of course, one of the others could lead, but it's up to the family not to let them down like that.

The next verse is well in the tavern tradition of the 'Little Brown Jug, how I love thee'. Having poured contempt and scorn upon the improvident females who so recklessly squander precious grain for drink, he looks round while he is playing his *Timbila* and, glancing under his arm, he finds to his dismay that the bottle by his side is empty! This line never fails to raise a laugh.

From time to time the various districts seem to undergo periods of strained relationship. Someone or other of one district may have transgressed against a member of another and the whole community of that area is consequently under restraint at the hands of its neighbours and is liable to be set upon if unwise enough to trespass on their land. This verse seems to refer to one of those occasions when the people of Filippe Banguza were unpopular. Their two neighbours, the districts of Zavala (here called Zaline) and of Nyabindini (Nyakutowo's district), lay between them and the Administrador's office at Quissico. Here also on the hill at Quissico overlooking the lakes by the sea was situated the office of the Witwatersrand Native Labour Association, where men would have to go to sign on for the Rand mines, having first obtained their exit permits and passport photographs at the office. So how are they going to get there if the way is closed? Dawoti, the native clerk at the office, says they will have to go off to the W.N.L.A. office some twenty miles to the west at Manjacaze, outside their district, in the opposite direction, in the area called Muchopes. Manjengwe, the messenger of Zavala, and his heir, is appealed to as a fellow musician to be reasonable, or how will they get to Chamusi, the labour office?

Anyway, this Administrador, Ngungundwane, is always calling them to go to the office and they cannot disobey him, so they will just have to go across those districts and risk being set upon. The feud did not last long, they say, and had blown over by the end of the year and the right of way was restored.

The painful subject of corporal punishment on the hands is now mentioned again. Katini made it the theme of his 7th Movement in the 1940 *Ŋgodo, Joosinya Cibudo Combidi*, when we commented on it in detail (p. 15). Now Katini's sentiments are supported by Gomukomu, coupled with a straight objection to the fact that the sentences are carried out by a Chopi, Julai (English 'July'), the head sepoy who does not even hesitate to smite 'the Lord's anointed', the chiefs. Anyone who has passed through that nerve-straining experience will appreciate the remark and require no further elucidation over the matter of the trousers. But Julai, the head sepoy, imagines that this painful business gives him superiority over the chiefs he is instructed to chastise; he thinks it entitles him to 'open a book' on his own account! The book referred to has nothing to do with our colloquialism concerning four-legged beasts but is the book of names kept at the Administrador's office for each chief, showing the roll of villagers and all taxable persons. Julai perhaps has dreams of reward for faithful service, faithfully carried out in every detail even to the beating of the women's hands. As a matter of fact, Julai is a particularly fine and trustworthy sepoy who is a credit to the service in which he is engaged and only carries out his plain duty. It is rather against the practice of hand-beating in general than against Julai himself in particular that the poets of the country direct their protestations on behalf of those at the receiving end of the rod of justice.

The incident at Sewe, which is one of the local names for the small and picturesque port of Inhambane, refers—like Katini's

PLATE V

At Chisiko there were two clowns, one dressed as a leopard and the other a python. They stand between the orchestra and the line of dancers. The Python Clown is beyond the Leopard, facing him

PLATE VI

The Rattle Players take advantage of the moment to do a few solo dances (*Kutsatsula* action), while the dancers crouch poised for the next move. A moment in a dance at a mine compound. At Banguza's village the dancers crouched right down like the single dancer in the centre of the line

1940 Ŋgodo—to the visit of President Carmona to the colony. The Chopi musicians having played at one big *indaba* at Magul were taken off by train to play for a second one some 200 kilometres to the east near Cape Corrientes. Something went wrong with the commissariat, and on their arrival by the narrow-gauge train from Inharrime, tired and hungry, there was no food to be had and they went to sleep that night filled only with wrath. Gomukomu felt they had been let down and that, as the music-makers of the show for the President, they had at least earned their eats. What the truth of the matter is I cannot say. Anyhow, who cares, now you know the real cause of all this fighting—the beautiful Tsewane.

8th Movement. NSUMETO. Preparation for the Councillors
> *Wuhokile impwebwe!*
> *Wavawona wasikati vaŋgweno vasaŋgile mbo randa vakoma.*

> Cider time has come!
> So women nowadays favour the chiefs!

Cider time has come, it is November again and the fruit of the Cazhu-nut tree is ripening on the hundreds of trees which dot the whole country-side along this coastal belt. Everyone is collecting the fruit and pressing the long-awaited cider. Everywhere is carnival, and those first in with their cider are giving parties and inviting all the chiefs. Oh vanity of all vanities! These women are the same everywhere, chronic social climbers!

9th Movement. MABANDLA. The Councillors
> *O! Mata mazambi akubomba,*
> *Mata mazambi akubomba ŋgu timbila.*

> Oh! Here come the fine young men,
> The fine young men for dancing.

The *Mabandla* movement is dramatic because it is danced in two sections. The dancers who up till now have danced together in one line now split up into two sections which, in the old days, used to represent, they say, two sets of opposing councillors. André Fernandes, in the sixteenth century, described the dancers dividing in this way and dancing against each other in mock attack and defence actions.[1] It must have been an early form of

[1] Appendix I, extract from p. 142.

Mabandla, the Councillors, and still to-day the fine young men of the Chopi tribe turn out in all their finery of jackal skins to dance the latest version of the *Ŋgodo*, the Chopi Ballet. They dance to-day to new music and new poetry composed afresh every year or so. But it is interesting to know that the musical genius of these people has remained unbroken for four hundred years, a record of an enduring passion.

The fine young men who line up for the dance are quite distinctive. You could not mistake them for Zulu, Shangaan, or Sotho; they have a cast of feature which is easily recognizable. Their heads are narrow and finely drawn with long, thin noses curving evenly to their nostrils and unlike the more usual flatnosed Bantu types. They seem to have something of the Watussi or Semitic type in them, though their history shows no such contact. They hold their heads well with a proud tilt upwards, and a line of these strong young men all six foot or more swaying to the music of the *Timbila* is a grand spectacle.

10th Movement. YOKUGWITISA YEŊGOMA. *The Drum Finale*

This movement has an almost unbroken accompaniment of drums as in the 'Entry of the Dancers', so poetry again is out of the question.

11th Movement. MSITSO WOKATA KUGUMIRO. *The Orchestral Finale*

This, as in all the *Migodo*, is a repeat of the 1st Movement, the *Msitso wokata*, and ends a fine performance, outstanding for its musical intensity and virility, its surging dances, and its keenly humorous and pointed lyrics. It has established Gomukomu's position as one of the most gifted of living Chopi musicians.

5. ŊGODO

Composed in 1941 by Sauli Ilova, orchestral leader and composer at the village of Chief Chigomba Mavila, Zavala District

MOVEMENTS

1. *Mutsitso wokata.*   First Orchestral Introduction.
2. *Mutsitso wembidi.*   Second Orchestral Introduction.
3. *Ŋgeniso.*   The Entry of the Dancers.
4. *Mdano wokuita.*   The Call of the Dancers.

THE LYRICS: POETIC JUSTICE

  5. *Mdano wakusinya.*   The Second Call.
  6. *Cibudu.*   The Dance.
  7. *Nkata Mdindo.*   The Song.
  8. *Mabandla.*   The Councillors.
  9. *Njiriri cinoteka.*   Dancers' Finale.
10. *Mutsitso kugwita.*   Orchestral Finale.

They say that the name *Nkata Mdindo* for the 7th Movement is the same as *Mzeno*.

1st and 2nd Movements are the usual orchestral introductions composed by Sauli Ilova. He is a quiet kind of man with unprepossessing features and clean-shaven head. He is not a naturally cheerful person, which may account for the lack of humour in his lyrics. He has seen much domestic tragedy which is reflected in his verses, but nevertheless his music is good and he commands respect for his ability as a leader of his orchestra at Mavila's kraal.

3rd Movement. IJGENISO. *The Entry of the Dancers*

    Mwamna waŋgu gwamba womba gukulewa.
    Mwamna waŋgu gwamba womba gukulewa.
                                    Iŋgoŋgo wako.

    My husband will tell m₁ when he's drunk.
    My husband will tell me when he's drunk.
                                    You bitch!

This somewhat crisp little piece of human understanding bears a familiar ring in any language, a 'just you wait 'til I get you alone' sort of touch. Definitely an unfair advantage, he thinks, and so bursts out with the concluding invective which is as well translated as maybe, though somewhat blunter in the vernacular. A stimulating little verse to bring the dancers in with, one would agree.

4th Movement. MDANO. *The Call of the Dancers*

    Lavanani ita bayeta,
    E bayeta kamukoma Cigomba, Matikiti yowanduwuna.

    E bayeta kamukoma Cigomba, Matikiti yowanduwana.
    Meseriani waMiceka ndinduna natahombe toŋgola mafu.

    Meseriani waMiceka ndinduna natahombe toŋgola mafu.
    Hinaruma Hurimbwini dana Canule icaŋga eta bayeta.

    Hinaruma Hurimbwini dana Canule icaŋga eta bayeta.

Hiŋganibfa hidanwe Cigombeni
Iŋgahoma 'Mbo dia' majaha hinaŋga tibva kunyeneswa.

Hiŋganibfa hidanwe Cigombeni
Iŋgahoma 'Mbo dia' majaha hinaŋga tibva kunyeneswa.

Uaŋgoti Makarite nete Bubwane
Uaŋga tawa 'mbo dia'.

Uaŋgoti Makarite nete Bubwane
Uaŋga tawa 'mbo dia'.

Uanatsula Cisikwini tailani hica bayeta.

Uanatsula Cisikwini tailani hica bayeta.

Camosi waŋgu udatwe majaha kulowa
Mfana waŋgu wo yafela matini.

Mfana waŋgu wo yafela matini
Ufete garini kamati epwata mhlambili mfane yowaŋgu.

Ufete garini kamati epwata mhlambili mfane yowaŋgu.

Wanefanisile mweno okawe
Waŋga mitambula kudelwa mfana waŋgu.

Waŋga mitambula kudelwa mfana waŋgu,
Mfana waŋgu, he-i, Cigombane nawiyelwa gucani.

Mfana waŋgu, he-i, Cigombane nawiyelwa gucani.

Natsula ndicadana Matikiti
Atanivuna kusaluka mfana waŋgu ulowile.

Natsula ndicadana Matikiti
Atanivuna kusaluka mfana waŋgu ulowile.

Mekuluŋgwane yatiŋgamu hagovani
Sekani sakwanu metukaleka mfana yewaŋgu.

Mekuluŋgwane yatiŋgamu hagovani
Sekani sakwanu metukaleka mfana yewaŋgu.

Lavanani ita bayeta
E bayeta kamukoma Cigomba, Matikiti yowanduwuna.

Come together and hail,
To hail the Chief Chigomba, Matikiti deputizes;

To hail the Chief Chigomba, Matikiti deputizes.
Meseriani of Micheka is also an important person.

Meseriani of Micheka is also an important person.

We shall send Hurimbwini to call Chanule so we can hail him.
We shall send Hurimbwini to call Chanule so we can hail him.

THE LYRICS: POETIC JUSTICE

Just listen to the songs of Chigombe's village,
To keep on saying 'Good day' is a nuisance.

Just listen to the songs of Chigombe's village,
To keep on saying 'Good day' is a nuisance.

Makarite and Bubwane are in prison
Because they did not say 'Good day'.

Makarite and Bubwane are in prison
Because they did not say 'Good day'.

They had to go off to Chisiko to say 'Good day' there instead!

They had to go off to Chisiko to say 'Good day' there instead!

My Chamosi is dead, my lad.
They look for my child in the water.

They look for my child in the water.
He drowned in the lake and no one could save him.

He drowned in the lake and no one could save him.
They trouble me these people.
They were the death of my child.

They were the death of my child
My child, alas, Chingumbane! What can I have to replace you?

My child, alas, Chingumbane! What can I have to replace you?
I will go and call Matikiti
Who will help me mourn for my child who is dead.

I will go and call Matikiti
Who will help me mourn for my child who is dead.

The women wept by the lakeside,
Only you who have no sorrow can laugh. O my child!

The women wept by the lakeside.
Only you who have no sorrow can laugh. O my child!

Come together and hail,
To hail the Chief Chigombe, Matikiti deputizes.

Here we have an almost classic example of a Chopi lament. It is difficult for us to understand why there should be all that irrelevant matter before the lament begins. We would have started right away with the verse 'My Chamosi is dead, my lad'. But his own private sorrow is a sorrow to be shared with all the village, with the affairs of the village, and in any case, it is a good thing to get the chief to share your mourning. How true this is even for ourselves, who arrange great gatherings for our funerals.

So Sauli Ilova starts his lament by including a statement about the situation apropos the chiefs and elders of the place and a recent case they had been involved in.

It appears that the old chief Chigomba Mavila is too old to take his full share in active political and social life. The head-man or *induna*, Matikiti, has for several years been acting as chief in almost everything but name. This Matikiti is a strong character. He is short and stocky, with a good forehead and a well-kept pointed beard. He is a quietly spoken man and gives you the impression of being a cultured person. These factors are both his making and his undoing. He is the very man a European would tend to trust and the Administrador has found him reliable and the natural head of the village. But the old chief who, they say, is not such a strong character, is jealous of him and of the fact that the people naturally turn to Matikiti rather than to him in time of trouble. In October of 1943, the old chief, who was not expected to live much longer, had issued an ultimatum to the Administrador that he would not die in peace if 'that man Matikiti' was not banished from the district instanter. This threw everyone into a fix. No one could deny the hereditary right of the old chief to have his wishes fulfilled, but equally, no one for a moment doubted where the real strength of the village lay in spite of their unswerving loyalty to the royal house. When I left the district the problem was still unsolved, whether Matikiti was to accept temporary banishment to appease the old man, or stay and risk being accused of attempting to usurp the chieftainship as well as bringing down Chigomba's grey hairs in sorrow to the grave. It was another of those moot points which an already overworked Administrador could well have done without. I have not heard the outcome of the affair yet, nor if there were still further complications thrown in afterwards. But enough has been said to account for the peculiar relationship of Chigomba Mavila, the Chief, and his *induna*, and the bracketing of their names in Sauli Ilova's opening sentence. Meseriani of Macheka seems only to be a make-weight in this affair and I have not quite fathomed who he is. Like Chanule, he seems to have been a friend of the composer and worthy of a big 'How-di-do'.

And talking of 'How-di-do's', what a nuisance it is to have to greet everyone with a 'good day'. It has become so overdone in these parts that it sounds like a kind of new song at Chigomba's village! One thing about Matikiti, he is a stickler for etiquette, and particularly with the white men. I imagine he knows which side his bread is buttered and these little things make all the difference. Anyway, Makarite and Subwane would not conform in this matter. They had even refused to come when the chief called them, and had been sent off to the jail at Chisiko (Quissico) to cool their heels for a spell and learn how to mind their 'good days' in the confinement of their cells. That will teach them to greet people politely in future! 'Good-day!'

Now comes the lament, the tragic event which has so clouded Sauli's horizon and left him without an heir. By putting the whole event into his *Mzeno* the people would dance his lament and everyone would share it. The story, so Majanyana explained to me, was this. Chamosi Chigumbane was Sauli Ilova's only son. He was about nine or ten years old and still herding the goats. He and his other friends herding goats with him had gone off down to the lake as they always did, but on this occasion they had challenged him to a swimming contest—who could swim out the farthest. Chamosi went far out ahead of the other lads and then they lost sight of him for a moment. He called out, but they could not get to him. What happened then they do not know. They tried to find him, but they were only small boys and the water was well out of their depth. One of them ran back as fast as he could go to the village and called the women, and a girl went quickly to fetch his father, but by the time he got there the women were keening beside the lake and it was too late. For days Sauli searched through the tall reeds that grew along the lakeside, but not a sign of his son's body did he find. The lake had claimed him utterly and all for a childish contest of skill. What folly to play with Fate like this, to dare his only son to a needless death.

He would go off and talk to Matikiti about it all. He was a man who would understand—understand what it is like to lose your only son, the lad Chamosi.

5th Movement. MDANO WAKUSINYA. *The Second Call*
    Tulane msindo votsi UaCopi,
    Hiŋgani butana mincaŋga taapfa Mdano.
    Tulane msindo votsi UaCopi,
    Hiŋgani butana mincaŋga taapfa Mdano.

Oyo Mdano waSiwana Miniti unako edaisa.
Oyo Mdano waSiwana Miniti unako edaisa.

Amawe Miniti wotileka timwane unako hidaisa
Amawe Miniti wotileka timwane unako hidaisa.

Iŋgahigela vasihora nana
Ibombelo yacani yotimbisa sibayane?

Iŋgahigela vasihora nana
Ibombelo yacani yotimbisa sibayane?

Mileka magwadla nowosiwana wacibayane cahambanza?
Mileka magwadla nowosiwana wacibayane cahambanza?

Dzokoruwana nimkumetwa naiceka nikopwata nimkuluŋgwane?.
Dzokoruwana nimkumetwa naiceka nikopwata nimkuluŋgwane?

Tulane msindo votsi UaCopi,
Hiŋgani butana mincaŋga taapfa Mdanao.

Stop your noise, all you Chopi,
Come together and hear the *Mdano*!
Stop your noise, all you Chopi,
Come together and hear the *Mdano*!
Oh that *Mdano* of Siwana Miniti distresses us.
Oh that *Mdano* of Siwana Miniti distresses us.
Cease, Miniti, it tears out our hearts.
Cease, Miniti, it tears out our hearts.
Tell us, you girls,
Why do you mark your temples?
Tell us, you girls,
Why do you mark your temples?
Why not use bangles and not cut your foreheads?
Why not use bangles and not cut your foreheads?
Dzokoruwana, why did you leave me with no one to talk to?
Dzokoruwana, why did you leave me with no one to talk to?
Stop your noise, all you Chopi,
Come together and hear the *Mdano*!

It is not stated in the text just what quality it was in Siwana Miniti's *Mdano* which tore out their hearts, but I was given to understand it was not discordant but the opposite, a fine piece of music which held them in its grip. Discords, incidentally, are hardly possible in the whole minor-tone scale to which their instruments are tuned. They may play wrong notes which they call *Madiyo*, but the tonality of the instrument is altogether most concordant, *Kudiŋgana*.

In this village of Mavila, which is only about five miles away from Filippe Banguza, they also show signs of moving with the times and objecting, like their neighbours, to the girls marking their faces and bodies. The age-old custom may well be on its way out if the young men of the tribe continue to object to it. Sauli Ilova, who is a travelled man in so far as he has been to Johannesburg and seen other tribes working on the mines, has come back with constructive criticism, remembering perhaps the Venda or the Zulu women who wear ankle bangles and do not mark their faces. From our own point of view, we must admit it would be a step in the right direction, and if the ankle bangles were anything like those of some of the other African women, a very musical step to the jangle of the bangles.

But the next verse brings us back to poor Sauli's domestic affairs again. His wife deserted him at one stage of their married life and so left him an empty hut to go back to at night. In this almost entirely illiterate community, illuminated by no reading-lamp, conversation remains an art and a constant solace. Oratory and lyrics, not study and literature, are the social arts of their village life. It is in fact quite necessary at times to call upon them to let up on their conversation, if only to turn their attention to their other passion, music.

6th Movement. CIBUDU. The Dance
Hiŋganyeŋgisa varurela vatsulaku kwawe, vaŋgati ko tava ciŋgamula vana-zumba mtini.

Awa Cigomba, hutano ketwe hiŋgalawa poŋgo ucilawa ŋgombe hinaŋga dila Paruki.

Hinaŋga dila iTowane micileka nyani misikati wavane vati kudaiswa mikuwo vateku mkana Matikiti.

Ndikondela ubarakile kudaya mwanana wavane asonacilo uteku mgisa cibowa.

Hiŋganyeŋgisa varurela vatsulaku kwawe, vaŋgati ko tava ciŋgamula vana-zumba mtini.

Listen, they are off to their kraals as they are afraid they will be signed on.

You, Chigomba, go fetch a goat and a cow to mourn the death of your mother Paruki.

We mourn Towane, but not his wife, because she always said she would kill Matikiti.

Ndikondela, you have troubled them by killing their child who had done you no harm, yet you poisoned him with a toadstool.

Listen, they are off to their kraals as they are afraid they will be signed on.

The tentacles of the W.N.L.A. stretch far out into the countryside of Africa. There are few places you can go in the southern part of the continent where a W.N.L.A. representative has not been before you. The Witwatersrand Native Labour Association is an efficient organization and is controlled by a number of strict regulations which ensure that recruits shall not be forced to walk long distances or be herded too closely into overcrowded trains or ships. Other regulations insist upon a large proportion of their wages being kept back from the labourers so that they will not squander all their money before they get back home. The balance is paid to them in full when they return to their own district. All the same, advantage or no advantage, economic pressure upon them to sign on for a spell on the mines is considerable, though for the most part their heart is not in it. So when the recruiting officer is about, anxiously trying to fill up his tally, it is best to make yourself scarce or you will find yourself being talked into it again.

Sauli Ilova is off again on his mournful touches. The old mother of the Chief Chigomba Mavila has died and the minstrel reminds the old man of his common duty to the dead, and incidentally to the living who will decently and willingly, if not exactly gladly, help him taste a little mutton and beef in memory of the old creature. After all, it is expected of a man in his position.

Then there were two more deaths recently, the man Towane and his wife, both of them within a few days of each other. He was a good fellow, Towane, but his wife never liked Matikiti; she never trusted him and believed he was up to no good with the chieftainship. She didn't hold with that, whatever the old Chief Chigomba was like, and she did not hide her feelings either. She'd kill Matikiti, she said, if ever she could lay her hands on him. Well, now she comes to die first, you can't really be sorry for her. She herself wished Matikiti ill. But it was a blow to both of them, Towane and his wife, when their child died, you must allow, and they do say it was that fellow Ndikondela.

Ndikondela did not turn a hair when he heard all this. He was not guilty, you see. So Sauli's shot in the dark missed fire.

7th Movement. NKATA MDINDO. *The Song*

Uleka Mjeŋgwe awe Misiri, unawayelwa ŋgucani unandizaŋga.
Uleka Mjeŋgwe awe Misiri, unawayelwa ŋgucani unandizaŋga.
Meseri unawusa wusiwana wusina'mpeto.
Meseri unawusa wusiwana wusina mpeto.
Mfana waPapatani wuka kuſaŋga.
Mfana waPapatani wuka kuſaŋga.
Hiŋgakuſaŋga wasiora nana uto ugwitelwa.
Hiŋgakuſaŋga wasiora nana uto ugwitelwa.
Aŋga mpwata kamsudi wakwa barama.
Aŋga mpwata kamsudi wakwa barama.
Mwanana wako wamweyo ŋgaŋgole.
Mweno Mawilana mwanana wako wamweyo ŋgaŋgole.
Lavanani waNkanda miciteŋgisa.
Lavanani waNkanda miciteŋgisa,
Miciteŋgisa tamfana weCilini.
Miciteŋgisa tamfana weCilini.
Fortini waMakatacilo kudana mako uciteŋgiso Mzeno.
Fortini waMakatacilo kudana mako uciteŋgiso Mzeno.
Ucitapfa Mzeno kaCigombo-o.
Ucitapfa Mzeno kaCigombo-o.
Makatako akudimba panzopfu!
Makatako akudimba panzopfu!
Utolo vete kuruketelwa ŋguva koma.
Utolo vete kuruketelwa ŋguva koma
Vanyosilanu! Iŋgadaya tate waŋgu unabuma puŋgo.
Vanyosilanu! Iŋgadaya tate waŋgu unabuma puŋgo.
Hetsuleni cikwaŋgwa nzani kaMahaſulana,
Hetsuleni cikwaŋgwa nzani kaMahaſulana,
Hicamana wakaMakatacilo nakuita gokuparela.
Hicamana wakaMakatacilo nakuita gokuparela.
Nina uya gumusana nikata milayo.
Uleka Mjeŋgwe awa Misiri, unawayelwa ŋgucani unandizaŋga.

Why not seek the advice of Manjengwe, Misiri? You are too wonderful.
Why not seek the advice of Manjengwe, Misiri? You are too wonderful.
It would be a shame if we starved.
It would be a shame if we starved.
The son of Papatani is leaving his home.
The son of Papatani is leaving his home.
Girls, this is not desertion but poverty.
Girls, this is not desertion but poverty,
He has not even a tree to shade him.
He has not even a tree to shade him.
He has but one child like a 'Possum'.
You, Mawilana, you have only one child like a 'Possum'.
Come, you people of Nkanda, and hear.
Come, you people of Nkanda, and hear,
Hear about Chilini's boy.
Hear about Chilini's boy.
Fortini, son of Makatachilo, call your mother to come and hear the *Mzeno*.
Fortini, son of Makatachilo, call your mother to come and hear the *Mzeno*.
She will hear the *Mzeno* of Chigombo.
She will hear the *Mzeno* of Chigombo.
You've got shoulders like an elephant!
You've got shoulders like an elephant!
You're always in trouble with the chiefs.
You're always in trouble with the chiefs.
You scabs! You are the ones who beat up my father because you thought you would get away with it.
You scabs! You are the ones who beat up my father because you thought you would get away with it.
It is said we should go to the diviner Mahushulana.
It is said we should go to the diviner Mahushulana.
If we should find the people of Makatachilo there we would kill them on the spot.
If we should find the people of Makatachilo there we would kill them on the spot.
And talk it over when we got back.

THE LYRICS: POETIC JUSTICE

Why not seek the advice of Manjengwe, Misiri? You are too wonderful.

Majanyana, who explained all these poems to us, was not very sure about this one. He knew only the bare outline of the details, he said, and would have to ask Sauli Ilova to explain. Unfortunately this has not yet been done, so for the time being we must be content with the explanation as we have it.

It appears that Misiri set himself up to be something of an expert in the growing of rice in the moist ground near the lakes and in the meadows. But his crops one year were not so good as they might have been, while Manjengwe's, from the Paramount Chief's area nearby, had been much better. Misiri had advised against early planting and a failure of the late rains had nearly ruined the whole crop. Manjengwe over the way had planted early and reaped quite a good crop. This Manjengwe was the musician friend of Katini at Zavala's village, who died in Lisbon in 1940. So it appears that this song must have been composed sooner than the others, possibly during the early part of 1940, and included in Sauli's new *Ŋgodo* which was first played and danced in 1941.

Mawilana the son of Papatani seems to have been one of those unfortunate people for whom nothing goes right. He was always hard up, his hut was in a bad situation, his fields were always the ones to be smitten with whatever scourge was about, and his wife had only managed to bear him one small child, undersized and undernourished. What a Jonah! Yet he seemed to be a nice enough chap when you knew him. So now he had to leave his wretched wife and child to fend for themselves while he went off to earn some cash as a labourer.

They say this 'Possum', *Ŋgaŋgole*, is a small, short-tailed animal with a long nose, and is uniparous, having its young only one at a time. It is a dark furry creature which plays possum by lying down on its back with its mouth open, pretending to be dead. Then when insects creep inside, it snaps its mouth shut and eats them. I have not been able to identify this creature for certain, but it seems to be the elephant shrew-mouse, also called *Nyagole*, or *Ŋgole*, about which there are many folk-tales in Africa.

What it was that Chilini's boy had distinguished himself for is not quite clear. It was suggested that he had done something particularly meritorious up at the mines, like saving life, in which both the people of this district of Chigomba Mavila and the people of Nkanda, the villagers of Nyakutowa near Quissico, were concerned. Here again Sauli Ilova himself must provide the answer.

Fortini (English tradition again 'Fourteen'), son of Makatachilo, was a strapping youth who was an enthusiastic dancer but by no means the best in the village. So he is picked out to go and call his mother to watch him dance and hear the *Mzeno* song, the *Nkata Mdindo*. In this movement there is more singing than dancing, and as he has a reputation of always being out of step, galumphing about with his great shoulders like an elephant, perhaps this movement would do him more credit in the eyes of his parent than some of the others. He was always throwing his weight about in other directions too, and was constantly getting into trouble with the authorities.

The next verse is not to be taken seriously; they say it refers to a bit of fun between some of the dancers at Mavila's village and those of Makatachilo nearby in Zandamela's area. 'You scabs!' is almost a literal translation of a common term of invective, though the Chopi refer to the pus below the scab. It had been suggested that the dancers of Mavila should go off and consult a diviner to find out how to defeat their rivals. So if their Makatachilo friends had had the same idea and got to the diviner first they would fall upon them on the spot, the blighters! Those fellows would do anything if they thought they would not be found out! Why, they would even beat up your father!

8th Movement. MABANDLA. The Councillors
O, waDarule ukoma wakufuma guWatoŋga vamipele.
O, waDarule ukoma wakufuma guWatoŋga vamipele.
Tate, wafaniseka Matikiti vakukona watsu diswa Deragube makono.
Tate, wafaniseka Matikiti vakukona watsu diswa Deragube makono.
Cisakana cawundile cihasutwe.
Hambu uncinelamba nehokile.
Uci!
O, waDarule ukoma wakufuma guWatoŋga vamipele.

O, Darule, you have lost your chieftainship to a cloth-wearing Tonga.
O, Darule, you have lost your chieftainship to a cloth-wearing Tonga.

THE LYRICS: POETIC JUSTICE

Father, Matikiti is worried because they say he has been sent for to go to Delagoa Bay.

Father, Matikiti is worried because they say he has been sent for to go to Delagoa Bay.

Now the secret is out,

Whatever you do about it!

There!

O, Darule, you have lost your chieftainship to a cloth-wearing Tonga.

This Darule was a chief's messenger and was due for promotion to one of the lesser chieftainships. But he fell from grace in the course of his duties, how it is not stated, and his place was filled by one who was not even a Chopi but a member of the despised race to the east, the Tonga. They wear their garments of printed cloth in a special and characteristic manner which is rather old-fashioned in this part of the country where the Chopi miners have now taken to trousers.

The feud between the decrepit old chief, Mavila, and his chief councillor, Matikiti, caused a lot of amusement in the village. They call on the old man, mockingly, saying that his strong-minded councillor hears a rumour that he will be one of those called upon by the government of the province to go to Lourenço Marques (called by the natives *Deragube*, Delagoa Bay) under indenture to work for the Government Headquarters there, and he does not like the idea.

'Now the secret is out' is, literally, 'now I have pulled the bird's nest to pieces' so how can it be mended again? So there!

9th Movement. NJIRIRI CINOTEKA. Dancers' Finale

This movement is danced in two sections and represents attack and defence movements between the opposing parties. It appears to be more often the formula adopted for the previous movement, *Mabandla*, in other villages, but one does not expect absolute adherence to custom. Each composer likes to be original in his own *Migodo*. There is no poetry for this movement but only cries, called and answered, at the end of the dancing.

10th Movement. MUTSITSO KUGWITA. Orchestral Finale

As usual, this repeat of the opening musical statement ends the Ŋgodo of Sauli Ilova.

6. ŊGODO

Composed in 1941 by Sipingani Likwekwe, orchestral leader and composer at the village of Chief Chugela Chisiko, Zavala District

MOVEMENTS

1. *Nsitso.*   Orchestral Introduction.
2. *Nsitso wembidi.*   Second Orchestral Introduction.
3. *Ndano.*   The Call of the Dancers.
4. *Mzeno.*   The Song.
5. *Yakusinya.*   The Dance.
6. *Yakusinya wembidi.*   The Second Dance.
7. *Ndindo.*   The Song.
8. *Mbandla Moyiso.*   The Councillors.
9. *Mufoŋgolo kugwita.*   Orchestral Finale.

It will be noticed that this *Ŋgodo* is rather shorter than the others, and the naming of the various movements is not the same. There is no *Ŋgeniso*, Entry of the Dancers; the *Mzeno*, usually the seventh movement, is fourth, and its place is taken by one called *Ndindo*, like the *Nkata Ndindo* of Mavila's kraal. The eastern Chopi dialect is apparent here in that they call the Introductions *Nsitso*, and the Councillors *Mbandla* instead of the more usual *Mabandla*. This *Mbandla* they make the last dance which is also unusual, as there is generally one more movement for a Dancers' Finale. Then again Sipingani has an original name for the Orchestral Finale in *Mufoŋgolo kugwita*, although it is only a repeat of the opening *Nsitso* as with all the others.

This village reflects in no uncertain manner the inadequacies of its chief, in all its behaviour and even in its dancing and music. Sipingani himself is a good musician but he cannot hope adequately to control his orchestra or dancers in this ill-disciplined place which compares unfavourably with the others.

1st and 2nd Movements. NSITSO *and* NSITSO WEMBIDI. *Orchestral Introductions*

These, as usual, contain no poetry.

3rd Movement. NDANO. *The Call of the Dancers*

Hiya-ha-hi! Hiŋgani yeŋgisa, eyo masinjita!
KaVinici Mapepe vadi kuvuma.
Tipoŋgo taŋgu mwa 'bii' ŋguMawewe ni mapaŋga.
Eyo Masinjita kaVinici.

PLATE VII

The dancers leap into their dance. The *Kukawula* dance routine is most energetic with high leaps and kicks and swinging of spears and shields. Dancers at a Witwatersrand Mine Compound

PLATE VIII

At a Witwatersrand Mine Compound

The dancers advance in line with swinging gait towards the orchestra in order to sing their 'great song' in the *Mzeno* movement, the climax of the *Ngodo*

THE LYRICS: POETIC JUSTICE

Hiya-ha-hi! Where are we going, what surprises!
Vinichi says Mapepe has been made Chief.
My goats are finished—*bii*[1]—by Mawewe, and also my bottles.
Oh, the surprises of Vinichi!

This somewhat disjointed little song is made up of statements which to the locals are all amusing and to the point. Vinichi is a noted wag and has a reputation of passing somewhat startling remarks. Who, for example, could possibly for a moment have believed that Mapepe had really been made chief? He is well known as a sycophant of the worst order, hanging around the chiefs and gossiping. But in these days, with the present chief, why, anything might be a change for the better.

Mawewe also has a reputation for hanging around where he is not wanted, and then things mysteriously disappear, goats and bottles of cider, for instance. But thank heaven, we have Vinichi to keep us amused sometimes.

4th Movement. MZENO. The Song
Uacilawanani ni vakatano makono hefila migela fidilo.
Σidilo cinikunaco mwana Nyakudima wadi kunisumulula.
Kuteka nemwanana wafawa tinyume ŋgene Cilenje.
Matuwane waŋgu wapwata nekulwala.
Matuwane waŋgu wapwata nekulwala.

Awe, Cugela, woteka newukoma ucibaŋga ŋguwona weciluŋgu.
Ukoma bwaNyaligolana neCugela!
Ukoma bwaNyaligolana neCugela!
Asiwanawo guli gaUani.
Kusoteka komwako woCugela acikawe anakuluwe.
Sitiki adikusiwa makuŋgoni vaci kahenzivi
Nditi kodo ndaMawewana ndati iyimbi.

UakaNyakumaŋga hi taŋgide kunyanowa icamba mambe gene mamo Cugele.
Aŋgateko neimpiŋgwe Wakanzila acagobenula.
Munu muNyalegolane wandombe ndiyo wabenula.
Cugele ŋgulava ŋgaŋzu unateka.

Awe Sipiŋgane woteke nekuraya
Ucafavisa ŋgufela kusela tisope.
Tomvu yakulamba huta ndiceya njovu cimansadi raya.

[1] The Bantu have many expressive onomatopoeic words such as *bii*, which are quite untranslatable. This one is usually accompanied by a quick movement of the hand from one side to the other in front of the mouth.

F

Madina awa Tsabweni akwanda ŋgutu maya kutala.
Udiŋga raya Tuyani neCihaŋgalani kutsala kutsapele.
Nkoma kani Karai uwi gumi rembwa.

Kuyandiga neme ninatsa ne ŋguhayi nicapetani mulekambiyani.
Ninaŋgarukwa ndidzaŋga wacago wani hambo niti kunini,
Nerukwaŋga ŋgusi koroka sakukumba kale meso sobaŋga
Sotekani nemisisi icidulekela gukona kubaŋga.
Kudila mwanana awaŋgu Matuwane waŋgu.

Naŋguwita kuweleka makono nakonole mwana yaKudima, nditsuri neŋgakumba,
Niŋgapwata nekuruma Matuwane waŋgu, mwanana waŋgu gutsenda waloi wadade.

Come together with your wives and I will tell you of my mourning this year,
Of the bereavement that I, the son of Nyakudima, have suffered.
You have taken your child, they say, and sold him for monkey-nuts, Chilenje.
My Matuwane never was sick.
My Matuwane never was sick.
You, Chugela, you are proud of your position, yet you are only a chief made by the white men.
Oh the chieftainships of Nyaligolana and Chugela!
Oh the chieftainships of Nyaligolana and Chugela!
It is a shame that should be hidden from Wani.
Chugela is always asking presents from his brother.
Sitiki is excluded from the council. They say they don't know him.
The country of Mawewana is full of troubles.

You of Nyakumanga district started yesterday speaking about Chugela.
The people of Wakanzila took the presents and kept them.
The son of Nyaligolana also took them away.
But Chugela wants the uniform and he will get it.

You, Sipingani, you take the post and sell it
To get something to drink.
'One can never smell danger ahead like the elephant.'
The name of Tsabweni is legion yet they go on using it.
Name your children Tuyani or Chihangalani and so on.
You, Karai, are you a mulatto?

If I go to the mines, where shall I find the courage to get into the cage?
I was once upbraided by women who were fetching wood and water,
Even by an old woman, so old she was already deaf,
So old she was bald.
Mourn my child, my Matuwane.

Do you say I will get a child this year, son of Kudima? I miss my
   child so.
He had hardly begun to fetch and carry for me, my Matuwane my
   child, before he was taken.

This lament was composed by Sipingani for a friend of his, Chilenje. Chilenje had asked him to do so in order to mourn for his child Matuwane. So Sipingani made up this *Mzeno* for him and set it to music, as if it came from the mouth of his friend. He even goes so far as to make fun of himself in the fourth verse to complete the illusion that it was Chilenje's poem. The sorry state of affairs in their district is also stressed as a cause for regret.

It appears that Chilenje was a cripple who had lost one leg below the knee in a mine accident. He had difficulty in getting about and so his small son Matuwane was a great blessing to him, fetching and carrying for his father. He felt himself to be rather a burden to his family. He could do no useful work for them and he overheard, from time to time, unkind remarks from the womenfolk about his uselessness. So when Matuwane, his child, died suddenly after a very short illness it left him feeling that the light had gone out of his life. He longed for another child to replace his Matuwane. It was his one bright hope for the future which otherwise must have seemed hopeless enough with his body crippled for life. This is the main theme of the lament.

To take the poem verse by verse. . . . It is not clear what is meant when they accuse Chilenje of selling his son Matuwane for monkey-nuts. Majanyana, our translator, could not enlighten us, so this must be left to Sipingani to answer.

This district of Chief Chisiko, incorrectly spelt in Portuguese as Quissico, gave its name to the village where the Administrador of the district has his headquarters. The office is situated upon a spur of the hills overlooking the long chain of blue and bottle-green lakes which separates the village from the dunes and the sea beyond. At the foot of this range near the lake-side is Chisiko's village among the palms and the Cazhu-nut trees. It is one of those unfortunate districts which has run into difficulties over the question of succession. The chieftainship has changed hands several times under Portuguese guidance, but now the line has worked itself out into a family whose two sons are both mentally deficient. The question before the Administrador is whether to depose the present line and appoint a better man, or whether to leave the situation as it is in the hope that matters will right themselves in good time. It is not an easy problem. In the meanwhile both the Administrador and the people know that the district has gone to pieces under the stupid boy who is legally their chief and the weak old relative who acts as his chief councillor. Chugela Chisiko is the name of the young chief and Nyaligolana is his councillor. The strong man of the sub-tribe, Sitiki (English 'Stick'), could no doubt have helped pull things together, but Nyaligolana was jealous and obtuse and kept him out of the councils. No wonder Sipingani declares it is a shame that should be hidden from the Paramount Chief Wani Zavala, particularly as the old chief in days gone by was one of the finest in the land, they say; a shame that the line of the great Mawewana should peter out in this ignominious way. It can only be hoped that if the children of the present chief do not improve upon the mental abilities of their father, a change will be made. That, it appears, is the general feeling among the people of the district, and as such must needs find popular expression in the songs of its musicians, 'for the country of Mawewana is full of troubles'.

What the presents referred to in the third verse were is not certain. They may have been the courtesy presents brought to a chief upon his accession or when cases are settled by him. Whatever they were it seems that they fell into the wrong hands and were divided among those who had no right to them.

Now Sipingani points a finger at himself and pretends he has stolen the letters out of the post to get money to buy drink. He is no tippler, though no doubt it has been known before now that someone has tampered with the mails, particularly if it was known that many of the grimy and well-fingered envelopes with their scrawled addresses contained a few hard-earned pounds sent home by a nostalgic husband from the womanless barracks of the mine compounds. Drink is an evil in this district, they say, though it would be unwise to make comparisons with other parts of the country in which the problem may be equally severe and equally long-standing, if we remember what André Fernandes had to say about it. In the Cazhu fruit season the cider is certainly a preoccupation for a few short glorious weeks, but for the rest of the time the usual Kaffir beer made of fermented grain and the imported red wines are available in the villages or at the Portuguese and Indian stores at a price. The wise old saying of the country-side quoted by Sipingani as a warning to wantons—'One can never smell danger ahead like the elephant'—does not perhaps refer to the elephant's reputed inability to forget but rather to that animal's acute sense of smell which warns it of danger in the wind. Robbing the mails must be one of those sins which inevitably find you out in the long run.

The Chopi, it seems, like many other people, have popular crazes for certain names, which run in cycles. The name Tsabweni has become as common as Jack or Anthony with us, and the poet begs parents to show a little more originality.

Karai comes in for a reprimand in a single sentence tacked on to this last verse, short and to the point. Karai has a reputation, they tell me, for running about from chief to chief wanting to be a somebody everywhere, instead of staying quietly at home like a proper villager and waiting to be asked. A proper villager does not go to chiefs outside his own district and offer his services to them as well as to his own chief. But mulattos who have no solid foundation in either camp are known for this very thing; feeling neither the freedom of the governing race nor the restrictions of native family life they are not constrained to attach themselves with loyalty to either in a single locality. They are, sadly enough, the victims of this twilight region of instability until one or other of the forces uneasily yoked within them takes charge and leads them into calmer ways. Such behaviour is not seemly for a Chopi, Karai!

The tragedy of the physical risks entailed in all mining operations by the men at the rock face is well expressed in this account of the young man brought home without one of his limbs, a useless body, dependent upon his already-overworked womenfolk, feeling his uselessness and clinging to the hopes he has built up around the small lad, his son, who dies just as he had begun to be a loyal little companion to his father. Although the record of mining accidents is creditably low, yet by the very nature of the work accidents must continue to be experienced, and the lifelong payment for the risks has to be met by those few who are unlucky enough to be chosen by fate to bear them. Here in the villages there are no institutions or cripple homes. The victims of accidents must be carried by their people as a part of the family responsibility, an unproductive hungry unit in the family economy. No wonder Chilenje feels mortified by the hard words of the women upon whom he now wholly depends, he who had to summon up all his courage each day to get into that mineshaft cage to work thousands of feet down below ground. And all he gets is a certain sum in compensation and the knowledge that he is useless for the rest of his life. One cannot help wishing that the son of Kudima had the right answer for him.

5th Movement. YAKUSINYA. The Dance
Hote dila ibane wakaSakati, iŋgacaŋguda Magudele.
Haŋga ndila Camukwe Caŋgunda.
Wasikati waCisikwini kaNsakatini, Jopela watu, ŋgu maha mabemba.
Nyamadowo watati waŋgu gumadibemba aleka kudideve Ndiganini.
Cilalane mbu kwinya-kwinya weneŋgela sope apwa kowukoma wuŋga hoka
Hote dila ibane wakaSakati, iŋgacaŋguda Magudele.
Haŋga ndila Camukwe Caŋgunda.[1]

We mourn for ourselves, we of Sakati. Speak for us, Magudele.
We mourn for Chamukwe Changunda.
The women of Chisiko and Sakati, Jopela our son, are very silly.
Nyamadowo, son of my father, has gone and left his money at Ndingani.
Chilalane goes to and fro drinking and saying, 'The chieftainship is within my grasp!'
We mourn for ourselves, we of Sakati. Speak for us, Magudele.
We mourn for Chamukwe Changunda.

The village of Sakati, they tell me, is the second most senior in the district of Chisiko. The people mourn for the death of one of their sub-chiefs. The woman diviner Magudele plays an important part in their lives as a clairvoyant and soothsayer. It is the custom of Europeans to deride and underrate the function of diviners in African village life, but my experience of them is that they are far nearer the sooth, or truth, in so far as it applies to their small community, than we usually give them credit for.

The domestic affairs of the women of the two villages of Chisiko and Sakati are not explained nor why his brother should have left his money at Ndingani, though this may have referred to some portion of a marriage settlement. Majanyana could not enlighten us. But the short word sketch of the roisterous figure of Chilalane is perfect in itself.

[1] Each verse, except the last, is repeated twice.

They mourn for themselves, these unhappy people of the Mawewana district; nothing ever seems to go right for them.

6th Movement. YAKUSINYA WEMBIDI. *The Second Dance*
Anyaŋgu naidulisa yawe.
Anyaŋgu naidulisa niŋgata dawa ŋgu mwana waŋgu.
Natsula kamugodini kugadila nateka tipondo nitafawa sope nicinina tasela.
Nila wako lumbane Mbilane adi kunilamba.[1]
I'll have done with this doctor,
I'll have done with this doctor as I fear I shall be blamed by my man.
I'll go to the mines to work for money so that when I come back
    I can buy cider to drink.
I want my darling Mbilane who has turned me down.

The first verse is supposed to have been said by a woman. She had been going to a certain herbalist for remedies of which she knew her husband would disapprove when he came back from the mines. From what they say, it seems as if the case was equivalent to one of us disapproving of a woman's going to consult a tea-cup reader.

The second verse is well in the tavern tradition, reminiscent of our sailors who sail away to a far countree to come back home with their pockets full of gold and court the pretty Polly. Only in this case it is the buxom Mbilane.

7th Movement. NDINDO. *The Song*
VaSakatini neWadiŋganini
VaSakatini mofela cani wukoma bwavane?
Wadiŋganini mudaŋga waleke vana ŋgafuma
Vadikudimana ndikombo ndakuteka mafu wacibanda kwenye
Vaciwaniŋga Vanzileni.
Σeŋgetile cawuya kambe
Cibando wufaka
Cawuya kambe
Cibwakile.
Miciwawona Wakisisi hambu vaBilobia vadanini
Ŋgoko wacihifula ni navaniŋga ifana waNderagube.
Malema akona kudiha fikweneti
Hambu kuteka ditoŋga nicidi hakukuna mahuŋgu.
E-e! Hiŋgane malala!
Hiŋgane nzera nteka vakaSakati
Ŋgatu vaCisiku.

[1] Both verses repeated twice.

The people of Sakati and Wadinganini,
Why do they fight about their chieftainship?
You of Wadinganini, let them be Chiefs.
They have taken the country, we know not how, and shared it out
Even to those of Wanzileni.

They have quarrelled again,
The friends have quarrelled.
We have come again,
Here we are.
If you see those people of Wakisisi or Bilobia, call them.
Because they played *Timbila* better than us, we should like them to
    play against that boy from Delagoa Bay,
For it is a rule you must pay your debts
Even if we must pay with a Tonga.

He-e! Be still!
Let us hear the news from Sakati,
Especially from Chisiko.

Here again the preoccupation of the district over their chieftainship is the subject of their song. But this time the musician has had enough of all this wrangling. 'Let it alone,' he advises the people of Sakati and Wadinganini. 'After all, it is the affair of the Europeans, the Portuguese who took our country long ago, we know not how, and made chiefs away from the legitimate line of succession, even sharing out the country to such people as those of Wanzileni.[1] Well, what do you expect anyway? We can't settle it ourselves, so leave it to the Government,' he suggests.

Now for a happier topic, the playing of *Timbila*. We must admit that those musicians of Wakisisi and Bilobia[2] played better than we did and we must pay up like men, even if we have to pay as in olden times with a Tonga slave.[3] But all the same we'd like to see them play against that lad who is now working in Lourenço Marques. He's a better musician than any of them.

But in the meantime, let's hear the latest news in this eternal squabble from headquarters at Chisiko's village.

[1] The people of the Zavala sib are called Wanzileni, 'of Zileni'. Their right to the paramount chieftainship has been challenged from time to time, and the dispute appears to have arisen a century or so ago.
[2] The native names of two mining compounds on the Reef.
[3] See André Fernandes again, Appendix I, p. 144.

8th Movement. MBANDLA MOYISO. The Councillors
    (Cries by the Dancers before the movement begins.)

Lawavhela isa ŋgweni
Vhela watu nkosina.

  Lawavhela isa ŋgweni
  Vhela watu nkosina.
  Uyo baleka Ŋgungunyana, naŋgu Mavulendhlovu.

Indhlovu idhla miti
  Indhlovu idhla miti.
Σaiyani 'Haeti'
  Haeti!

Leader. The people approaching the gate
         Say, 'Do you want us, Chief?'
Men.   The people approaching the gate
         Say, 'Do you want us, Chief?'
         See Ngungunyana flees, here is Mavulendhlovu.
Leader. The elephant eats trees.
Men.   The elephant eats trees.
Leader. Cry Hail!
Men.   Hail!

    Hakulo-ora kusika timbila,
    Hakulo-ora kusika timbila.
    Sipiŋgani waLikwekwe ndi bemba.

    You must dream to compose music,
    You must dream to compose music.
    Sipingani of Likwekwe is carried away.

    The traditional cries are similar to those that used to be chanted by many Bantu tribes before battle and are now commonplace in dances. This one, said in the Shangaan tongue, refers to the great native wars in this part of the world, those between the Shangaans and the other tribes, from whom they took the far side of the Limpopo river on their way up from Zululand when they failed to subdue the Chopi, and to the defeat of the Shangaans by the Portuguese ending in the battle of Magul near the Incomati river.[1] It was there on 8 September 1895 that their famous chief Gungunyana was finally beaten after a lifetime of filibustering and brigandage. Mavulendhlovu was said to have been one of his captains.

[1] The name of this river is spelt with a *k* on the South African side of the border and with a *c* on the Portuguese side.

For this last song, Sipingani the composer returns to his music, the joyful music of the *Timbila*, which thrills all true Chopi. Like Gomukomu, the composer at Filippe Banguza, Sipingani knows that you must have inspiration to compose new music for the *Timbila*. 'Just you watch me, I am transported with musical inspiration!' He says this with a smile in his eye. Sipingani, like his fellow musicians of other races, is not fool enough to believe his own publicity literally, but there—a little publicity is a good thing for us musicians now and again!

9th Movement. MUƒOŊGOLO KUGWITA. Orchestral Finale

This movement, which ends Sipingani's *Ŋgodo*, is the traditional restatement of the opening orchestral number. His music contains many attractive melodies, but cannot be compared with the compositions of either Katini or Gomukomu for depth of musical intuition. The unhappy atmosphere of their lake-side home in Chisiko's village without firm leadership from the Chief seems to reflect itself in all their undertakings. At least the poet and composer Sipingani attempts to fulfil one of his most important roles by criticizing the state of affairs, and the affairs of the State. By making his people sing their views he helps to restore the situation, if only by preparing the minds of the villagers for a change if and when it should come. We see the musician in this light as an important aid to essential law and order, without which no community can achieve even moderate happiness.

7. ŊGODO

Composed by an unknown composer, or composers, of Chisiko's kraal

This *Ŋgodo* was composed, they say, up on the Rand mines for dancing in the mine compounds. In all probability it borrows much of its music from a number of *Migodo* at home, though from the context of the poetry much of it refers to compound conditions. The Chopi all agree that music and poetry composed away from home are never as good as the genuine village music, nor are the substitute instruments they have to play on so resonant as their home-made ones. This I have corroborated from personal and independent observation.

On this occasion the *Ŋgodo* was being performed at Chisiko's village as a kind of junior *Ŋgodo* for training young children to dance, sing, and play their parts. It was staged after the performance of the usual dance composed by Sipingani. The orchestra continued to play for the children, and a number of young boys were allowed to come into the orchestra and play some of the instruments. The dancers were all youths between the ages of eight and fifteen with the exception of a few experienced dancers who encouraged and led them in the steps they should perform. Young girls took the minor parts usually allotted to their elder and married sisters, such as tenderly wiping the faces of the musicians and dancers when covered by perspiration in the heat of the moment, and dancing little jigs from time to time from the 'side lines'. It was the only occasion upon which I have seen a junior *Ŋgodo* performed, and it is not yet clear to me how the transition stage is overcome between the time when small boys are only allowed to perform the *Cimveke*, Pipe, dances and the moment when they are admitted into the ranks of the *Basinyi* and the *Uaveti*, the dancers and musicians. It is known that it demands a lot of practice, and in places you will find young boys, though never girls, practising upon roughly made *Timbila* called *Makokoma*, which are in reality loose slats of *mwehesu* wood cut to the right sizes and tuned to the same notes as the proper *Timbila*. These slats are placed over a small trench dug in the ground and are supported at either end upon rolls of grass or palm-leaf bound round a stick. They are played with light wooden beaters and make an agreeable sound quite good enough to practise on.

But to return to this Junior *Ŋgodo* which was led not by Sipingani but by Meneti Nzekani We Shutumba.

MOVEMENTS

1.	*Msitso Wokukata.*	First Orchestral Introduction.
2.	*Msitso Wombidi.*	Second Orchestral Introduction.
3.	*Msitso Woraru.*	Third Orchestral Introduction.
4.	*Ndano Kuŋgeniso.*	The Entry of the Dancers.
5.	*Mwemiso.*	Fast Dance.
6.	*Mucuyu.*	Dance in two Sections.
7.	*Njiriri Yokusinya.*	The Great Dance.
8.	*Mzeno.*	The Song.
9.	*Ndindo Womutsimedo.*	Dance in preparation for the Councillors.

10. *Mabandla.*   The Councillors.
11. *Msitso Wokukata.*   Orchestral Finale.

The meaning of the names of these movements is obscure and needs further investigation.

1st, 2nd, and 3rd Movements. MSITSO WOKUKATA, WOMBIDI, *and* WORARU. *Orchestral Introductions*

These opening movements, as usual, contain no poetry and are of the normal length lasting two minutes each.

4th Movement. NDANO KUŊGENISO. *The Entry of the Dancers*

In other villages this is divided into two movements, *Ŋgeniso*, The Entry of the Dancers, and *Ndano*, The Call.

Wambaŋgo,
Wambaŋgo mamaŋgisa valuŋgu sihihlute.

In battle,
In battle with the white men, the Europeans beat us.

These simple lines, repeated frequently while the young lads parade on to the dance floor in front of the orchestra, introduce the dancers to their part of the performance.

5th Movement. MWEMISO. *Fast Dance*

Magupancayo wati hosi.
Magupancayo kukozwala mazalo baiyete.
Hambidi muciŋgola valuŋgu kamihiheti cilo.
Mamwane majaha maŋgadi maſiita unzeno waWusapa.
Yeŋgenide ŋgonyama koponi kaMwazikiŋgi hiŋgateŋgisa.
Setelekana wemwana atu hiŋgateŋgisa harura.[1]

We sing the song of royalty.
We sing the song of the royal greeting.
Although you put some of us in jail, you white men, you will not finish all of us.
Other young men are still coming to hear the *Mzeno* of Wusapa.
There came a 'lion' into the compound at Mwazikingi. Come and hear.
They must go on strike, those people, on this account.

The Chopi frequently use their royal greeting which is similar to that of the Zulu *Bayete* or *Bayede*, and is usually *Haeyeti* or *Aeyeti*.

[1] All verses sung twice with the exception of the last.

THE LYRICS: POETIC JUSTICE

There is a touch of passive resistance in the second verse which takes courage from the happy knowledge that all the jails in South Africa are too small to hold everybody, so however many may be locked up at a time there are always plenty more coming along behind, and in the meanwhile what better recreation than to come and hear the *Mzeno* of Wusapa.

The next line refers to the arrival from home of a well-known and talented musician in one of the Rand mine compounds. They are always glad to welcome good players, and this compound of the Wit Deep near Germiston which they call *Mwazikiŋgi* or *Maskinki* was no exception. It is suggested that the native miners in the neighbouring compound *Mafuta* should go on strike there and come over to theirs in order to be near this great musician. Of course, if they did not appreciate him they could go away again. This 'lion' of the *Timbila* may possibly refer to Wusapa of the previous verse. This year the orchestra at Maskinki was in temporary eclipse for lack of players.

6th Movement. MUCUYU. Dance in two Sections

Ramba nani maŋganakana muciteŋgisa da maPortugezi zhani maluŋgwana hembaŋgo wamaTaliana.

Ramba nani maŋganakana muciteŋgisa da maPortugezi zhani maluŋgwana hembaŋgo wamaTaliana.

Maŋgomanyani wasika timbila.

Hedikwamana hacazumbela titavane.

Ɛawele mbaŋgo wavakoma waNkatanini

Wacazumbela sitolo.

Hilawa mfana waŋgu Silive
Adikuba mafaka ntembueni kuwatoŋga.
Kwacileŋguni hinaciwona cakwazumbela Pitoro.

Come together, you elders, and hear about the Portuguese and how the war goes with the Italians.

Come together, you elders, and hear about the Portuguese and how the war goes with the Italians.

Mangomanyani was composing music.

We found him sitting on the hill.

He was afraid of the meeting of elders of Nkatanini,

Who are waiting at the store.

We want my boy Siliva
Who stole mealies from the Tonga fields.
If we go to the City we see wonders as we pass Pretoria.

These Chopi work so much up on the Rand that they appear to associate themselves almost as much with the South Africans as with the Portuguese. The war with the Italians and Germans is naturally big news even if their country is neutral. They cannot escape the effects of war, but they can read its signs. Goods are not so plentiful in the stores, and they have heard stories of the fighting in North Africa. They have seen German and Italian submarines lying out at sea off their coast sunning themselves while they waited to attack merchantmen entering the Moçambique channel. They have even given hospitality to torpedoed passengers and sailors who have landed in out-of-the-way places along the wild dunes; they have collected flotsam from sunken ships, boats and deck fittings, and even bales of floating rubber, and taken them all, animate or inanimate flotsam, to the Administrador's office. Yes, the signs of war have swept along their peaceful coast.

What was it that Mangomanyani the composer had on his mind that made him avoid the elders? We do not know. We may never know. But it must have been something sufficiently heavy on his conscience to find its way into this song. Perhaps it may have had something to do with 'my boy Siliva' who stole mealies from the Tonga fields. But this does not make sense. The Tonga are fair game, and who cares if you do steal mealies from a Tonga? Only the unknown composer of these lines can enlighten us.

The forty-mile chain of mines and towns which is the centre of the Witwatersrand goldfield around Johannesburg is called by the Chopi *Cileŋguni*, the place of white men, and with its extent they are familiar. But the city of Pretoria, to them *Pitoro*, is an interesting town on the way to the mines from their homes. They do not alight there as they are almost without exception indentured for the mines some thirty miles farther on. With the exception of Lourenço Marques, Pretoria would be the only town of any size that a country-born Chopi would see on coming to work on the Reef for the first time, so reference to this phenomenon is not surprising.

THE LYRICS: POETIC JUSTICE 81

7th Movement. NJIRIRI YOKUSINYA. *The Great Dance*
    O—hisi O! Hiŋgapfa Mzeno!
    O—hisi O! Hiŋgapfa Mzeno!

    O—sing O! Listen to *Mzeno*!
    O—sing O! Listen to *Mzeno*!

This very short line frequently repeated is all that is sung in this movement which accompanies a most energetic dance.

8th Movement. MZENO. *The Song*
Hawuyesa!
Haŋgawekelu wamaŊgisa nimaBuni nemaPortugezi.
Hawuyesa!
Haŋgawekelu wamaŊgisa nimaBuni nemaPortugezi.
KwaΣiluŋguni naya guhayi nitava neŋge kuwilwa.
Didiho dekolo daŋgu nikusu kudamba
Waŋgu kuteŋgisa mihumbo.
Didiho dekolo daŋgu nikusu kudamba
Waŋgu kuteŋgisa mihumbo.
Siŋgavulela sihumide Sikotci majaha sakawa
Sinahoma mitsikari sifavulela.

Here they come,
Here they come, the English, the Dutch, and the Portuguese.
Here they come,
Here they come, the English, the Dutch, and the Portuguese.
How can I go to the city since my finger is cut off?
I have been compensated, so I am glad.
They say I may feel pain in it.
I have been compensated, so I am glad.
They say I may feel pain in it.
We have allowed the young 'Scotchmen' to come . . . they have danced till they swooned.
They say they danced till midday.

Here is another brief glimpse into the everyday affairs of the mine-worker. One has had his finger amputated after an accident, and the mine doctor has warned him that the nerves may still give him trouble after it has healed. The compensation in cash seems to have satisfied him for his loss, but perhaps he feels somewhat self-conscious as yet about it, or, again, his hand may be too damaged to return to work at 'the Place of White men', *Σiluŋguni*. (In the 6th Movement, *Mucuyu*, it was called *Cileŋguni*. These variations often occur and one cannot tell which is more correct.)

The last verse has nothing to do with the Highland Fling. The Chopi, for some unknown reason, bear the nickname of 'Scotchmen' along the reef, and their love of dancing is notable. To stand up to the seven or more dance movements of the *Ŋgodo*, repeated twice over in the period of an hour and a half, needs both great energy and great enthusiasm.

9th Movement. NDINDO WOMUTSIMEDO. *Dance in preparation for the Councillors*

Madoda, madoda! Isaŋgo amile bonani?

> *Sikubonile, wena Blanketi! Uti 'Ndiya gula'. Mabalani wabuya watinina 'Sala pasi mufana. Wazofika minenjeni koponi.' Minenjeni koponi wabuya yatini 'Musunu kanyoko! Unxila kakulu. Hemboya goga!'*

Σaiyeni bayeti!

> *Haiyeti!*

Kwebelele . . . kwebele maciŋgana.

Cries.

Leader. Men, men! Didn't you see the gates?

Men. We saw you, Blanketi! You say to the clerk, 'I am sick,' and he said, 'Sit down, boy, the compound manager will come.' But when the compound manager came he said, 'By your mother! You are drunk. Go and dress for work.'

Leader. Cry Hail!

Men. Hail!

Song.

Kwebelele . . . kwebele maciŋgana.

This movement, which follows on swiftly from the one before, opens with cries of the call-and-answer variety. The words reflect a commonplace enough occurrence in any mine compound. The native feels ill and reports sick on parade. After a cursory glance by the compound manager he is pronounced a malingerer. So the old excuse has not worked again, and he must go to work, hangover or no hangover! The compound managers, they say, have a reputation for not mincing words, and it is a source of

PLATE IX

The Dance Leader brings in his men. He holds his dance spear and shield (see the shadow on the ground) and has his whistle in his mouth. He is wearing on his head baubles made from coloured wool which the Zulu call *Iziqhoma*, white vest, civet skin over his yellow loincloth, and angora goatskin leggings

PLATE X

'Oh! Here come the fine young men.' The entry of the dancers movement at one of the Witwatersrand Mine Compounds, with typical pointing gestures with shields and spears

envy how fluently they can sometimes string together the most unmentionable terms of invective. Such is life, and what do you expect of a compound manager anyway?

The words of the song's one line, they said, were taken from a Xhosa in the compound. They sounded well and so they put them to music, but they never got to hear what they meant. Who cares? They sound well.

10th Movement. MABANDLA. The Councillors
    O—hisi—O, hiŋgapfa Mzeno!
    O—hisi—O, hiŋgapfa Mzeno!

    O—sing O! Listen to *Mzeno*!
    O—sing O! Listen to *Mzeno*!

The words and music of this Councillors' movement that the young lads danced to were the same as those of the *Njiriri* movement. Up in Johannesburg, without their composers handy, they were no doubt hard up for music and so were forced to make use of this tune twice.

11th Movement. MSITSO WOKUKATA. Orchestral Finale

The *Migodo* for the young boys have to be finished off with as much ceremony as those danced by their seniors. So we find the orchestra completing the ballet with the traditional ending as before.

III
THE DANCERS AND DANCES

NOW that we have had a glimpse of the background out of which the Chopi poet conjures his lyrics, we must turn to the Dancers, the *Basinyi*, who sing them for him between the various complex movements of their own dance routines.

The *Basinyi* as a rule are all young men between the ages of about sixteen and thirty-five or forty, though it is not unusual to find older men still enjoying themselves by taking part alongside their juniors. On one or two occasions I have seen, carried away by the moment, men so old that I feared for their blood-pressure. One old man in particular I have in mind, a cripple who had lost the use of both legs below the knees in the mines. He wore pads on each knee and danced and shuffled half a dozen dances with the others. His body movements, though restricted, were so vitally alive and done with such evident delight that after the first few moments of misplaced sympathy one could only admire him. That was at Zandamela in 1940, and it illustrates the abiding delight these people find in their national pastime. At the other end of the line of dancers you are just as likely to find three- and four-year-olds with diminutive sticks and toy shields doing their very best to keep step with older brothers, with tongue seriously twisted between their teeth and with a fixed expression of concentration until they catch your eye and hurl themselves back into the shelter of their mothers' skirts in the crowd of spectators.

'The fine young men for dancing', as Gomukomu describes them, are certainly a distinctive and distinguished group among Bantu peoples. Their physique may best be described as lissom, rather above the average height of southern Africans, and with a characteristic type of head, narrow and long, with more bone to their noses than most. In old age, when their teeth begin to show gaps in their ranks, they lose much of their handsomeness and often become quite ugly. Their womenfolk, partly on account of their cicatrices, the 'marks on forehead and temple' and over their bodies, and partly from their slight build, are demure and, indeed, plain in comparison with the four-square buxomness of the Zulu women, for example.

When they dance, the young men dress in customary fashion, if they can afford to do so. This consists of a length of lemon-yellow cloth, *muceka kahalani*, wound round their waists, generally over short trousers, upon which chevrons, rather like the arm stripes of our military non-commissioned officers, are sewn. The forty or more years' acquaintanceship with the mines has converted them to European clothes and their bodies are in consequence unsuitably clad in a motley variety of undervests, shirts, or even football jerseys of the striped kind. Luckily much of this incongruousness is concealed under the jackal-skin cape, *didowo*, which they wear over their shoulders. The whole skin has a slit in the centre of the back and is placed over the head with jackal head in front and tail behind. Black feathers may be worn in a tuft on the head, but are not usual, as they are also used as a sign of mourning. The legs from below the knees to just round the ankles should be covered in white goatskin leggings, *siwaka*. Some dancers will wear monkey, civet, or goat skins, hanging from their belts as well as the yellow cloth. If you have one it is also correct to wear an armlet, *dicowa*, of long hair from the tail of a bullock or horse above the right elbow.

In the left hand they hold shields, *ciklavaŋgu* or *kavi*, about 30 inches long, with which they bang the ground with a report like a pistol shot. In the right hand they may carry a stick, spear, or axe, but the most favoured dance-stick is a wooden spear-blade, *ditſari*, some 24 inches long, finely tapering to the tip from a broad base near the short handle.

Decorations are also worn, mostly medals won for special merit up on the mines, prominent among them being the red-cross badges which indicate proficiency in First Aid. Others also wear, quite irrespective of their intrinsic value, the remarkable gewgaws that may be picked up in any kaffir store. You will often find small mirrors among them to flash in the sunlight. So much for the costume.

The dancers, like the musicians, are led by one man, the dance leader, *Muniŋgeti wabasinyi*, sometimes called *Mbandi waMbandla*. This man is not only the leader but also as a rule the composer of the dance routines. When the music has been set to the lyrics the composer plays them over to the dance leader whose job it is to devise the dances to set against them. This means, in a *Ŋgodo* of usual length, a matter of six or seven different dances. As far as I know, no European has witnessed the beginnings of a new dance routine or watched the initial stages through which a dance leader instructs his dancers. It all comes so naturally and so quickly to them that they make light of it when you make inquiries. To them it is so perfectly simple that they find it hard to understand why we should want to know about something so obvious. It is clear to anyone who has seen many of their *Migodo* that the several dance leaders strive to get original effects and new patterns into their movements. No two *Migodo* are exactly alike, just as the music in each variation is different, and yet even in their dissimilarities they display the special and exclusive characteristics of Chopi artistic achievement. These they recognize as readily as we do our own. They are given to remarks as scathing as those we make ourselves about the monotony of foreign music and dancing when they consider they are merited, as in the case of the eternal *ho ho siyana* of the Shangaan songs. But the musicians I brought to Durban were most appreciative of the Zulu *Indhlamu* dances, though they admitted they were not 'in their line'.

The general characteristics of African dancing seem to persist through the centuries. The descriptions given in the sixteenth century by Father André Fernandes and Father Gonzalo de Silveira of a Chopi dance are applicable to-day to the *Mabandla*, Councillors' movement. The account by Father André Fernandes is to be found in his letters (see Appendix I, extract from p. 142). Here is the account of the same dances from the *Life of the Blessed Father Gonzalo de Silveira*. It was translated from the Latin into Spanish by Bernado de Cienfuegos, anno 1614, and translated from the Spanish by W. J. Cruddas in 1931. This translation is unpublished and was shown me at the Archives in Salisbury, Southern Rhodesia.

'They are fond of good music and instruments and love dances, in which they imitate their military exercises, sometimes soldiers besieging a city, other times soldiers besieged, and again splitting up into squadrons to attack the enemy, and so on in various ways.

'For these dances they dress themselves in skins of lions, tigers, and other wild animals, securing them in such a manner that as they spin round quickly on one foot, the skins fly out all round them to the great amusement of the spectators. When one of the dancers has finished his figure, before resuming his place in the ranks he raises so great a cloud of dust with his feet that he can scarcely be seen.'[1]

It seems probable that this account was taken from official documents or reports sent home by André Fernandes, as that busy and hopeful young priest Gonzalo de Silveira was only in the place a few days or weeks before he went on to his martyrdom in Monomotapa six months later. It is stated that he spent his time baptizing everyone he could get hold of, and 'he would have had no great difficulty with God's help, in casting out the devil from the kingdom, had he stayed longer'.[2] There can have been little time left for watching dances. Judging by the small matter of cider, the devil stayed all right, though not the priest.

So there is little doubt that many of the dance actions were founded upon warlike manoeuvres, even in the days of these pioneer missionaries four hundred years ago. The history of any African tribe must include as unbroken a series of wars and tribal struggles as our own. But it would perhaps be unwise to conclude that all dances performed by the young men are war dances or based upon the movements of soldiers. The fine young men for dancing are, of course, the fine young men for battle, and they would be expected to perform as a body both in their dancing and in their fighting. But since the occupation of their country by Europeans, tribal fighting has receded and the Chopi have not had to fight for several decades. I mention this because it is popular amongst Europeans to call all Bantu dancing 'war dances' in order to obtain a spurious satisfaction from watching the performances of those whom they would romantically like to call 'savage warriors'. Dancing was used in times past to instil *esprit de corps* into groups of men about to go into battle, and in the semi-trance state of the dance they would overcome their initial fears and act as a body. But the essential joys of dancing in peace-time have no such objective and are attained through

[1] Book II, Chapter IV, p. 11.
[2] Ibid., p. 17.

the sheer thrill of performing intricate manœuvres in perfect unison. Being out of step or making a mistake in the dance is always the cause of ribald laughter amongst the crowd, though we, with foreign eyes, often find it difficult to spot the fault or irregularity which gave rise to such spontaneous amusement. It is perhaps for this reason that some of the villages feature clowns in the *Ŋgodo*. The clowns do everything wrong and offset the perfection of the other dancers. At Chisiko there were two clowns, one dressed as a leopard and one as a python. They pretended to give battle and danced against each other with wild athletic leaps and gestures. They were exhausted long before the *Ŋgodo* was half-way through and retired from the scene, having fondly embraced each other, amidst general laughter from the onlookers.

Europeans find it difficult to estimate with any certainty the intrinsic value of a native dance. As spectators and not participants we are inclined to judge the dances from the visual standpoint because the movements and music may not evoke in us the desire to participate, and thus enjoy the satisfaction of sharing the ecstasy by sympathetic action. Now that we have long since forgotten how to express our common emotions in dancing, leaving the finer aesthetic side of the art to professionals, we are nonplussed by the spectacle of Africans who dance not only for joy but for sorrow, and in order to express or acknowledge religious emotion. Until we have the benefit of the researches of a man who can learn their dances and participate in them, we are unlikely to have an authoritative statement on the subject. But having participated, our research dancer may be able to convey to us a more authoritative appraisal of African dances than we have ever had. In the meanwhile only motion pictures with simultaneous sound track will in any degree substitute for the experience of the Chopi *Ŋgodo* as performed in its proper setting, under the big shade-trees of the villages of Zavala.

Without these mechanical aids I will only attempt to do what others have in the past found equally difficult, describe briefly what happens in each movement of two *Migodo*, one by Katini (1943) and one by Gomukomu (1943), of which the poems have already been discussed.[1] I quote my notes which were hurriedly scribbled while the performances were in progress. I have wit-

---
[1] See pp. 19 ff.; 39 ff.

THE DANCERS AND DANCES

nessed many performances and have made notes of a dozen or more. I find it possible to distinguish the movements by their style and also to remember the sequence of steps. But this, it will be admitted, is a very long way from knowing the dances as a dancer must know them, who has actually taken part in them.

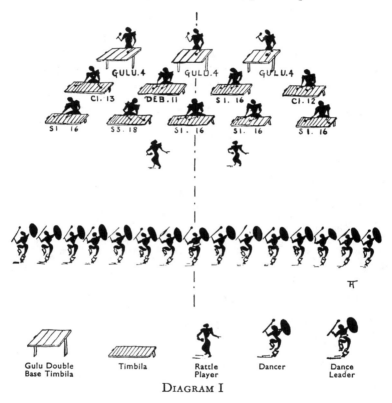

DIAGRAM I

I)GODO of Katini (1943)

Performed on 22 September 1943 at Zavala's village, Zavala District, Portuguese East Africa

Composer: Katini Nyamombe

Leader of the Dancers: Komichi Zumbi

The orchestra of twelve players, *Uaveti*, and two rattle-players, *Mdoto Wanjele*, was drawn up in the shade of the trees where they always play, just outside the village. The orchestra was set out in three ranks with the two rattle-players standing in front, facing in the same direction. Katini sat in the middle of the front row with his senior player Hafu (English, 'Half') on his left, each playing a *Saŋge*. The fifteen dancers, *Basinyi*, were preparing for the dance, fixing their jackal skins and leggings. They formed up in line opposite, facing the orchestra.

The Paramount Chief was present. Without being prompted he had thoughtfully had a table and chair brought out for me to write at, remembering my visit to his village for the same purpose two years before. He sat beside me and answered questions, explaining to me what was happening. When he gave the signal for them to begin, Katini led off the orchestra into the Introductions.

1st Movement. MUSITSO WOKATA. *First Orchestral Introduction*. (*Duration, 1 min. 45 sec.*)

Katini opened his *Ŋgodo* dramatically with a few swift strokes on his *Timbila*, *kuniŋgeta indando*, and the orchestra followed him into a stirring introduction, *kuvetani vootse*; after playing for about a minute, Katini gave the signal (*kuvelusa*) for the coda by playing three rising notes in octaves, *digando dimwedo kudiŋgana*, when the orchestra repeated the measure, *indando*, for the last time.

Then, after a pause of a few seconds, Katini gave them another few notes of introduction and they all played a single musical sentence lasting about ten seconds.

2nd Movement. MUSITSO WEMBIDI. *Second Orchestral Introduction*

This was a slow movement (180 pulses of the rattles per minute) started by Katini in octaves, with a single statement of the motive. The whole orchestra, with rattle-players, came in and played a very bell-like movement. Upon the indication being given for the coda, all the orchestra played a bar in octaves, after which there was an urgent accelerando to the end, which was marked by notes in octaves, *kugwita nedigando dimwedo*.

The dancers were now all prepared and lined up about ten paces away, facing the orchestra, though it is more usual for them to be drawn up to one side waiting for their entry.

During the playing of this movement I heard members of the orchestra singing words which I could not catch. When I asked

THE DANCERS AND DANCES

them afterwards what they had been singing, it transpired that they had only been singing sound-words to fit the notes of the melody they were playing. They started with *Nko nko nko*, for the three beats on the opening note of the measure. Other such words are *Nda, nda-nda tele, ndagalala tele telele*, &c.

3rd Movement. ƝGENISO. *The Entry of the Dancers.* (*Duration, 4 min. 45 sec.*)

Before the opening of this movement Katini by himself played over the melody in a kind of improvised cadenza, *kukata indando*. As a rule this is done solo, but other members of the orchestra, more especially the senior man sitting on his left, may add a note or two by way of punctuation.

When the cadenza was over, he started in earnest. This is usually as follows: he plays the opening cadenza, *kukata indando*, and merges it into a characteristic run down the instrument, *kusumeta*, which in turn merges into a statement of the motive, *kuniŋgeta*, which may be repeated once, twice, or three times before the orchestra comes in after the sign, *kuvelusa*, is given. A repeat of the measure is called *kuvagela*.

The entry of the orchestra, *kuvetani vootsi*, is the signal both for the rattle-players to use their rattles and for the dancers to start their actions.

In this case Katini introduced a slow movement (speed 152 pulses on the rattles per minute), and as soon as the orchestra entered all the dancers began their characteristic swaying from one foot to the other, two pulses on each foot (*llrrllrrllrr*), called *kuziŋginikela*.

They then sang the song in one short verse beginning *Ye Dawoti!* and as soon as it was ended advanced in line, *rirendu*, towards the orchestra, halting upon the last note of the movement about five paces away.

4th Movement. MDANO. *The Call of the Dancers.* (*Speed 240; duration, 2 min. 40 sec.*)

This fast movement was started by Katini with a fine descending cadenza, and when the orchestra came in the dancers began to sway, with occasional leaps into the air. They then began the action known as *kucuia*, in which the long-bladed wooden spears, *ditʃari*, and the shields, *kavi*, are pointed towards the right and left alternately. Then they all bent down and pressed their shields on to the ground in front of them, holding them there until Katini gave them the signal, *kuvelusa*, to begin their song. They then stood upright again and sang the song *Lavanani ʒentu Zavala*.

On completing the eight verses of the song, upon the last word of the last verse the dancers all turned left into file, *masuni*.

5th Movement. DOOSINYA. *The Dance.* (*Speed 200; duration, 4 min. 20 sec.*)

With a few rising notes Katini began the usual preliminaries during which the dancers showed great eagerness to begin the movement which is the first real dance. On the opening note, *kuvetani vootsi*, the dancers leapt into the typical Chopi dance which is called *kukavula*, and is most energetic. It is an exciting moment, and Katini, who is something of an impresario, began to wave his *Timbila* about in the air while he played. This he does by cleverly winding one leg over the arc of the instrument and gripping a leg of the *Timbila* between his toes. Then by leaning backwards on his small stool he is able to balance the instrument in mid-air while he continues to play.

After dancing a prearranged number of measures of this wild dance, during which they performed a set routine of steps, the dancers paused for rest by reverting to the quiet swaying movement on alternate feet, *kuziŋginikela*. This was repeated several times, the wild dance routine followed by a rest period.

Then at the signal given by Katini the dancers began to sing in unison the song *Aŋga kaMalanje*. Before the beginning of each verse Katini himself sang the opening word of the next verse.

As in the previous movement, the last note of the song ended both the song and the movement with the dancers turning into file.

6th Movement. JIBUDU. *The Second Dance.* (*Speed 248; duration, 4 min. 10 sec.*)

Katini led off with a very tuneful little melody in his opening cadenza. Then after his *kusumeta* he repeated the motive three times before the orchestra came in. The dancers began a quiet swaying motion, this time with single beats on each foot (*lrlr lrlr*). After a short while Komichi the dance leader rushed out

THE DANCERS AND DANCES

in front of them from one side, and this was the signal to start the *kukavula* dance as in the previous movement, but now it included another characteristic Chopi dance action, banging their shields on the ground in front of them, *kupeka hahatsi*. The shields hit the ground with a sound like a pistol shot and throw up the sand. In many Chopi villages it is easy to see where they dance as the shields have in the course of time worn out a shallow trench along the line of dancers. In other villages the ground is so sandy that much of the dancing is enshrouded in flying sand. Even André Fernandes mentions the play with sand.[1] Besides banging their flexible shields on the ground they also flip them against their forearms. The shield arm is thrown out with an under-arm sweep, and this brings the left side of the shield sharply on to the forearm. It must be painful, as I notice most dancers who do this protect their forearms with cloth or padding.

As in the last movement, the wild dancing alternated with periods of recuperation as they swayed *kuziŋginikela*. At the end of a routine, the dance leader called to them and as they swayed they sang the song, *Nzinda kaNyabindini*. While they were singing this song, one of the women in the crowd shuffled out sedately between the orchestra and dancers and returned to her place again. This shuffling parade by the women spectators is quite usual in many Bantu dances.

Then, at the end of the song, the dancers turned left into file upon the last note as before.

7th Movement. MZENO. The Song. (Speed 240; duration, 5 min. 58 sec.)

Before this movement started in earnest the leader, Katini, played over his melody, *kuniŋgeta indando*, and a few of his musicians assisted him with an occasional note and with humming and singing. With this over, and when Katini was satisfied that the dancers had got their breath back from the last two movements, he started the *Mzeno* movement. This movement is perhaps the most attractive to European ears. It is marked both by a change of tempo from fast to slow when the song begins, and by the fact that this is the only song sung without the accompaniment of the rattles, while the whole orchestra plays very softly, thus bringing out the full mellowness of the *Timbila* tone.

[1] Book II, Chapter IV, Appendix I, extract from p. 142.

Katini started the movement with a short introduction and the dancers came into a quiet, swaying dance. At a signal from the leader the dancers began to advance in line, *kutsula musuni*, towards the orchestra. After a few paces they danced again with pointing gestures made by sticks and shields, *kucuia*. They advanced again to within three paces of the orchestra and stood still, *ututa*, while the orchestra began to play more slowly and quietly. The effect of this is arresting. When the tempo had dropped to 180 the rattle-players put down their rattles and walked off to one side. Katini then gave the indication to begin the *Mzeno* Song, starting with the line *Hiŋganyeŋgisa*. The young dancers singing in unison made the song sound full and moving to the soft accompaniment of the *Timbila*. It was the lament to the musician Manjengwe. The verses are repeated twice and are separated by the playing of the measure by the orchestra alone. During the singing the dancers make appropriate gestures with their hands, *wasinya makara*, or mime the meaning of the words with one hand, *kusuŋgameta*, their spears being held in their shield hands.

Before the repeat of the last verse the orchestra speeded up the tempo to 240 again and played loudly, so that the coda was sung and played fortissimo. The rattle-players returned, quickly picked up their rattles, and beat time again while the dancers retired in line, *kuuya misana*, to their original positions. So the *Mzeno* ended, a movement of great beauty and musical power.

8th Movement. MABANDLA. The Councillors. (Speed 256)

Before this movement began the dancers uttered the traditional cries in answer to their leader. Komichi did a short *pas seul*, *ukulhokozela*, and then called to them:

Leader
   Abagwazi unyoko gubani?   Who stabbed your mother?
Men
   Yeti yaba,   We ourselves,
   Yeti yaba umcwayo.   We ourselves, the singers.
   Naŋgu waluŋgu wafikile   Now the Europeans have come
   Safuma Magijana.   They want Magijana.

Komichi again performed a solo dance and called out:

Leader
   Σentu!   People!

Men	
Zavala	Zavala
Mujaju	Mujaju
Watoveli	Of Toweli
Siyavela	We come
Sildya kwetu.	On our own.
Leader	
Zavale	Zavale
Men	
Zavála	Zavala
Leader	
Inya mwemele!	Each for himself!
Men	
Mwemele miri wakwe!	Each for ourselves!

The meaning of these cries is not clear. They may have come down from more savage days of intertribal warfare and it would require an intimate knowledge of the history of the people to understand them, particularly as they are spoken in Chishangana and not Chichopi. From what they said, I gathered that Magijana was the name of a Shangaan chief who lived on the borders of the colony near the Transvaal, against whom the Portuguese had sent out an expedition. Mujaju, they said, was a tribal god or ancestral spirit. The phrase 'on our own' was literally 'eating our own food', meaning independent of outside support.

The cries over, Katini immediately started the music for the *Mabandla* movement at a rattling pace, 256 pulses per minute. With the entry of the whole orchestra the dancers sprang to life and divided into two sections, one on either side of the centre line, *kubandwa*. This imaginary centre line divides the dance floor into left and right halves directly in front of the orchestra leader, Katini. The two sections moved off in opposite directions in file, *masuni*. When they had gone about 15 yards they turned about and came towards each other again. Now they advanced by taking four long paces forward and four short paces backward. When they met on the centre line the two leaders of the lines bumped into each other and they all turned into line facing the orchestra. The movement was now characterized by the dancing of pairs of dancers who broke rank and came out to dance in front, *kugavula*. The two dancers would dance in unison, starting at either end of the line, and dancing right across to the other.

When, eventually, they were called back into line by a blast on the whistle from Komichi, they performed one routine of the wild dance with high leaping, *kukavula*, and afterwards, as they swayed, they sang the words of the song *Wani Zavale*. The movement ended as previously upon the last word of the song.

9th Movement. NJIRIRI COKUGWITA. The Dancers' Finale. (Speed 264; duration, 3 min.)

This movement was even faster than the last and was preceded by a short *kuniŋgeta indando* by Katini during which five of the dancers came out and did solo dances, *kugavula*, and solo shakes, *makara*. These shakes are typical of Chopi dances. The dancer holds his arms out with elbows on the level of his shoulders, forearms hanging free. He then ripples the whole of his body swiftly from top to toe. The shake must require a completely supple body, and from our point of view I imagine is quite beyond the power of the ordinary mortal to perform!

As soon as they heard Katini preparing his opening cadenza for the customary start of the movement they ran back into the ranks and were ready to start the *kukavula* dance, followed by the *kuziŋginikela* swaying on alternate feet. Pairs of dancers came out of the ranks and danced together in front but retired when the orchestra began to play fortissimo. This indicated the start of the song, which was punctuated by a sharp clap on their shields with their right hands. They sang the song *Atuhakuwona*, ending the movement standing at attention on the last word.

Katini then gave them the opening note for the Portuguese national anthem which the orchestra played in unison with occasional beats on the Tonic *Hombe*.

After the anthem there was one blast on the whistle from Komichi Zumbi and the dancers broke off. The players, however, remained to finish the *Ŋgodo* by playing the orchestral finale.

10th Movement. MUSITSO WOKATA KUGWITISA. Orchestral Finale

This was played exactly as before at the opening of the *Ŋgodo* and fittingly ended the performance.

At their usual weekly dances this *Ŋgodo* would be repeated at least twice during the course of the afternoon. The different villages have different dance afternoons. Katini keeps Wednes-

THE DANCERS AND DANCES 97

days and Sundays as his dancing days from about 3 o'clock till dusk. They do not dance after that, he says, because his musicians need to see their instruments, though a month or so later he played for me by moonlight in Durban.

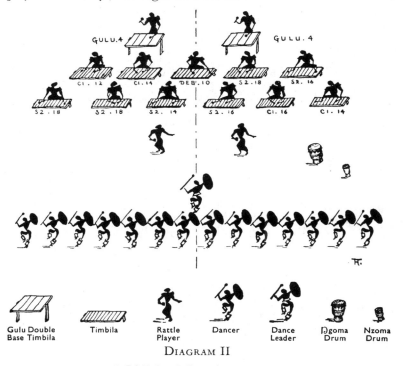

DIAGRAM II

ŊGODO of Gomukomu (*1943*)

Performed on 11 September 1943 at the village of Filippe Banguza, Zavala District, Portuguese East Africa
Composer: Gomukomu Wasimbe

This performance of Gomukomu's *Ŋgodo* was staged for me at the request of the Administrador. It was called for a day which was not one of Gomukomu's regular dance days, so many of his musicians and dancers were absent, though there were quite enough to make a good show. The orchestra of thirteen players were ready under the *mukusu* trees at the lower end of the village. Filippe Banguza, the chief, a powerfully built man of about forty, had a brick-built house farther up the slope which he later showed me. In it I found he had a *Timbila* of his own, as he himself had been a member of the orchestra before he took over the chieftainship and he liked to keep up his music even if he no longer played with the others.

The orchestra of thirteen players—from the possible twenty-four on regular days—was set out in three rows (see Diagram II). To one side were two drums, one larger one called *Ŋgoma* and the smaller one *Nzoma*, both single-headed open drums. The *Timbila* players, as is their custom, sat on small stools or logs of wood about 8 inches high. One of the players had an ideal stool in an old hippopotamus skull with the two top tusks still intact acting as the front legs of the stool. The natural curve of the skull made a comfortable seat.

The fourteen dancers and their leader, Gomukomu's 'fine young men for dancing', were now all lined up in their dancing kit already described, the leader standing a few paces in front of his men. Then at a sign from Filippe Banguza, Gomukomu started his latest *Ŋgodo*.

1st Movement. MSITSO. Orchestral Introduction in five parts

a. Msitso Wokata. First

Gomukomu led off with a short phrase, after which the orchestra came in in full strength and played the opening sentence, which ended dramatically on a rising sequence of notes. During this performance the dancers all stood still as they had no part in it.

b. Msitso Wombidi. Second

He started the second introduction with a cadenza, *kuniŋgeta*, the run down his instrument, *kusumeta*, and the introductory bar, *kuvelusa*. The orchestra then started and played a short movement. The excitement of anticipation got the better of one dancer who broke rank and did a solo dance, *makara*. The orchestra ended this piece in unison.

c. Msitso Woraru. Third

A few beats on the key-note *Hombe* by Gomukomu started this orchestral movement, which, like the others, was short, lasting only a minute or so.

At the end of this third introduction there was a diversion on the

PLATE XII

a. Ingalishi, maker of *timbila* xylophones

b. Chopi player seated on a hippopotamus skull stool

PLATE XII

Dance in progress in a Witwatersrand Mine Compound

One of the rattle players is performing a *pas seul* in between orchestra and dancers. The nearest dancer, who is possibly not a Chopi, is dressed as a clown. He wears a kind of wig, a Zulu *beshu* skin apron, and shoes. He carries a spear and stick in either hand

part of the dancers, who appeared to be objecting to something. I discovered they were complaining that one of the *Gulu* double bass players was not using his proper beaters with large soft rubber heads. He had left them at home and had had to improvise beaters of two sticks bound round with leaves and cloth. The player took the good-natured reprimand with what humour he could muster and they prepared for the next part of the Introduction. The incident will serve to illustrate the fact that attention to detail is a noticeable characteristic of the better musicians, and small matters which we might easily overlook are readily spotted by native artists and commented upon.

d. Msitso Womune. Fourth

After a cadenza in unison, octaves, by Gomukomu, all the orchestra played two notes in unison, *digando dimwedo*, and then started the movement. While they were playing two little boys of about seven or eight years old in the watching crowd came dancing out in front of the orchestra to do impromptu solo dances, but at the last minute their nerve failed them and they fled.

As the music ended the dancers shouted cries three times in response to their leader.

e. Msitso Woklanu. Fifth

The next started without delay, and while Gomukomu began a long preliminary cadenza, the dancers moved away in a group to one side to prepare for their entry. The orchestra joined in, the women began to warble their shrill cries, and some of them paraded in front of the orchestra. Again a dancer broke away from the others to do a solo *makara*.

The end of the fifth introduction was also marked by cries from the dancers in the 'wings'.

2nd Movement. *ŊGENISO. The Entry of the Dancers*

This movement was preceded by a long cadenza or improvisation by Gomukomu, who continued to play until he considered everyone was ready to start. The two drummers had taken up their positions at the drums and the dancers had formed up into file waiting for the indication to be off. The player of the larger drum, *Ŋgoma*, had two sticks for beaters with ends rounded into wooden heads, shaft and head all in one piece. The other player had two light straight sticks, and his small son, aged about six, was holding the little *Nzoma* drum firmly over his shoulder. His father stood or knelt behind him and beat the drum with swift strokes which must have nearly deafened the child. Against his regular pattern of light beats the player of the *Ŋgoma* played what syncopations he liked, using the fingers of his left hand to mute the drum and also to raise the pitch while the other hand continued to beat. But this drumming did not start until Gomukomu had brought in the orchestra. Then everything leapt into action together. With a swift double beat the drums cracked out like a cannon shot the precise moment of entry by the full orchestra and then almost overpowered the orchestra.

The dancers sprang to life and effected their entry by alternate pauses and short rushes in file. Once opposite the orchestra they turned, in obedience to their dance leader's whistle, into line, facing the orchestra. The leader himself took up a position a few paces in front of his men and directly opposite Gomukomu on the *kubandwa*, the centre line of the dance floor. As they advanced in line towards the orchestra, *kutsula musuni rirendu*, they sang the words of the song frequently repeated *Suŋgeta ŋguwo*. The movement ended with the dancers in their right positions some ten paces away from the orchestra.

3rd Movement. NDANO. *The Call of the Dancers*

There was a long cadenza and introduction to this movement, but when the orchestra began the dancers all sprang into the air and, as they landed, squatted right down without moving, awaiting the next indication for action. The rattle-players took advantage of this moment to do a few solo 'shaking' dances, *makara*. When the indication was given, the dancers leapt up and began an active dance with shield flapping and the pointing gestures with shields and spears, sticks, or ox-tail switches, alternately left and right, *kucuia*. At the end of a set number of bars they all pointed forward with their spear hands and rested. Then began the song with the words *Mahuŋgwa a Filipe*. Between each verse the orchestra played eight repeats of the measure *kuvagela*, during which the dancers continued their pointing actions, though while they sang they stood still, and towards the end of the song did their swaying motion, *kuziŋginikela*.

4th Movement. CIDANA CACIDOKO. *The Little Call*

After a brief cadenza and a one-bar introduction the orchestra followed Gomukomu into the music for a quiet dance. As they were dancing I walked along the line of players and listened carefully to each individual. They were playing at least four variations on the basic melody in the front rank alone. This is called *kudiŋgana*, playing in unison, or *kuhambana*, to play a second part in harmony with the theme.

The dance continued quietly, and at this moment the wife of one of the players came over to him from the crowd of spectators and tenderly wiped his face with a towel while he continued to play. This is not uncommon, as the weather can be very hot and the musicians most energetic. But whenever it happens I find this little action very touching to witness.

The dancers then sang the song *Lavanani miciteŋgisa*, which concluded the movement.

5th Movement. CIBUDO COOSINYE. *The Dance*

As its name implies, this was the first appearance of the energetic *kukavula* dance. Gomukomu introduced it by a short rising phrase, and at the entry of the orchestra, *kuvetani vootse*, at a very fast pace, the dancers suddenly crouched down on their haunches, appearing almost to collapse, and then raised their right spear arms in front of them. On the signal from the leader coinciding with a repeat of the musical motive they stood up again and started the quiet swaying dance *kuziŋginikela* (*llrrllrr*).

Then after the playing of a few measures Gomukomu gave his *kuvelusa* indication and with the next round the dancers started the wild *kukavula*. Further indications from the orchestra made the dancers change alternately from the *kukavula* to the quieter *kucuia* and back again until they had had enough. Towards the end of the movement they sang twice the short verse, beginning *Nizambwa nyekile*. After such energetic dancing it was all the dancers could manage. The verse for the next dance was even more brief.

6th Movement. CIBUDO COOSINYE KAMBE. *The Second Dance*

To a new melody the second part of the great dance started again after a few minutes' pause. The dance routine was virtually the same as the last, alternating the *kukavula* with the *kucuia* steps. They sang the two-line verse *Lavanani mootse*, and on the last note all turned left into file.

7th Movement. MZENO. The Song

It seems usual for the orchestra leader to play a long preliminary cadenza before this movement, no doubt in order to give his men time to get their breath before singing his great song, the *Mzeno*. The melody and contrapuntal playing of this movement, in particular, stamps its composer and players as musicians far above the average in almost any society, African or non-African. Subsequent recordings of this movement in South Africa have revealed the intricacy and splendour of this Chopi theme.

In comparison with the last it was a slow movement, and after a clever introduction the orchestra and dancers began their actions. The dancers advanced in line with swinging gait towards the orchestra and, as soon as they were within three paces of the players, they halted and stood at attention, *ututa*. The spectators, who had up till now stood behind the orchestra and on the two flanks only, crowded around the dancers and players on all sides. At indications given on the whistle the dancers performed a few measures of quiet swaying dance, *kuziŋginikela*, after which Gomukomu changed his tempo to a very slow one, from about 200 pulses per minute down to 144. The rattle-players stopped playing and put their rattles down, and the dancers held both shields and spears in the left hand, leaving the right free for gestures and miming. Now the song began with *Hiŋgane malala*, the dancers singing in unison and the orchestra playing very softly. In between verses they played rather louder with Sekelani, the *Cilanzane* player on Gomukomu's left playing the melody of each verse, *kuveta mapṣui*, on the top register of his instrument. The melody varies in subject and counter-subjects with each change of verse and is particularly attractive.

Between verses the dancers would sway and do a few quiet dance steps, and during the verses they would mime to give point to the meaning of the lines, pretending to raise a bottle to their lips in the fourth verse and turning their backs and walking away a few steps in the seventh. Each verse was repeated twice, which meant the singing of over fifty lines of poetry. Between the repeats of the last verse the orchestra played fortissimo in contrast to the strictly piano accompaniment up till then, and the last verse was sung slightly faster and louder. At the end of the movement the dancers and spectators moved back into their original positions after a few call-and-answer cries from the dance leader and his men.

8th Movement. NSUMETO, or KWABALU SUMETO MABANDLA. Preparation for the Councillors

This movement was a kind of intermezzo to cover the period between the *Mzeno* and *Mabandla* movements, while the dancers were retiring to their positions and while the crowd made way for them by retreating to the flanks and behind the orchestra. The music was played by Gomukomu alone without the orchestra, accompanying a short song in which all the people, spectators, dancers, and players joined. The single verse was repeated several times with a playing of the motive in between each repetition.

The title *Kwabalu sumeto Mabandla* means literally to count, or mark, the melody of the 'Councillors'. But the melody was not the same as that for the 'Councillors', so one can only translate it as an intermezzo in preparation for the next movement.

This interpretation is supported by the royal *Ayete* cries which the dancers now gave in response to their leader. The association of the Council of Elders with the next movement appears to be sufficient to account for the use at this point of a greeting which is reserved for chiefs and elders only.

9th Movement. MABANDLA. The Councillors

At the start of this movement the dancers immediately divided into two sections, each going off in file in opposite directions on either side of the centre line, *kubandwa*. After they had gone about 15 yards or so they turned about and formed up into a single line again and began a short routine of the *kukavula* steps. They then all sat down and watched pairs of dancers come out and dance together, as well as a few women from the crowd. There were also several solo dances, *kugavula* and *makara*.

Then Gomukomu called them all to attention by playing a high descant upon his *Timbila*, whereupon the dancers quickly got up from the ground and danced two short *kukavula* routines, between which they sang the song *O! Mata mazambi akubomba*.

At this point two small boys keenly interested in playing the *Timbila* tried to come and sit amongst the players, their elder relatives, but were driven away.

10th Movement. YOKUGWITISA YEŊGOMA. *Dancers' Finale with Drums*

This movement, like the second, is accompanied by drums. During the rest after the last dance, the drums were prepared by hammering in the wooden pegs which hold and tighten the drum-heads. This time the little boy's sister came out to hold the *Nzoma* for her father. She was a little girl in the leggy stage, about nine or ten years old, and was rather taller than her small brother, so her father did not have to kneel this time.

When Gomukomu began his preliminary cadenza the drummers warmed up and tried out their drums. The members of the orchestra also added a few runs here and there to the tuning up, but all of them without hesitation stopped immediately they heard Gomukomu start his opening. Upon the *kuvelusa* indication, the dancers, drums, and orchestra joined in with gusto and the dancers started the *kuzinginikela*, swaying with single beats on each foot (*l r l r l r l r*). The *Ŋgoma* drummer gave a high leap into the air as he finished an intricate measure of syncopated flourishes. At the same moment the dance leader sounded his whistle and the dancers did a surprising action. They all knelt down and placed their shields in front of them on the ground with their spears or sticks on top of the shields, leaving both hands free for action. In this position, the apparently truncated dancers performed the shaking action, *makara*, which up till now had only been seen as a solo, with their arms raised sideways and their forearms and hands hanging. It was clearly more difficult to perform the *makara* in that position than when standing.

The music now began to get faster and the dancers, still on their knees, kept pace with it. The *makara* ended, and the dancers leant down and slapped their shields with their hands. Next they all picked up their spears or sticks and beat time with them on their shields. Again there was another accelerando and crescendo, and the movements of the dancers became still more violent, the tempo having risen to 260 pulses per minute. The music gathered momentum both in speed and intensity, until the dancers seemed carried away by exhilaration. Then suddenly the whole line of dancers rose from their knees, surged forward towards the orchestra, and the music ended with players and drummers striking a single note in unison and the dancers with arms raised crying *Ayete!* 'Hail!' A magnificent climax.

The dance was ended and the line broke up, but the orchestra remained to play the finale.

11th Movement. MSITSO WOKATA KUGUMIRO. *Orchestral Finale*

The short but noble measure of the opening theme of Gomukomu's *Ŋgodo* was now repeated and with it the whole performance was complete.

IV

THE PLAYERS AND THEIR LEADERS

IT is almost inevitable that the dancers should steal the limelight from the musicians. Their movements, their dress, and their singing all attract the attention of the spectator. But the Chopi know it is the players who are the more important. After all, the *Ŋgodo* is led by the *Musiki waTimbila*, and not the *Muniŋgeti waBasinyi*. As with us, it is the instrumentalists who are usually the better musicians.

It had been intended to publish this description of Chopi musicians fully illustrated by gramophone records of their music. This part of the publication must follow, for 'by their works shall ye know them'. No description of music can replace the actual experience of the sound. Even in Africa, where most Europeans have only heard Chopi music in the distance or casually at some Sunday dance at a mine compound, little comprehension of the music has penetrated into our essentially foreign minds. It requires an unusually developed and sympathetic hearing to break down the initial barriers of strangeness. The gramophone record enables you to hear more distinctly the constituent elements of the music if well recorded. With an orchestra of similar toned instruments this is particularly helpful, as the mono-aural microphone selects and emphasizes the nearest instrument within its directional beam. Yet gramophone records of African music require explanation before they become clear to most of us. This is no disgrace, for even trained musicians are, as often as not, nonplussed by the intricacy of the music and hardly know how to set about assessing it. Few European musicians in my experience have the patience to overcome that initial shock or stay to unravel the tricks and fancies by which the African musician achieves his effects.

The reason is clear: the two musicologies are so far apart and their conventions so dissimilar. Our musicians, on hearing African music, unconsciously attempt to reduce it to terms of our tonality and our notation. The instinctive reaction is to think how out-of-tune the Africans are with our tempered scale. It takes them quite a time to become accustomed to the African modality; and, all the while, the struggle to think of the music which is being performed in terms of a written score is uppermost in their minds. But to the African musician, of course, the question of writing music does not exist. Music to him is wholly aural, never visual. Our very terminology reflects the difference in outlook. We talk of high and low notes and place them higher or lower on the staves. The Chopi, like other Africans, speak of 'small' and 'great' notes for treble and bass, and many of their musical terms are biological similes. In Rhodesia their Karanga cousins constantly use such terms as 'the young girls', 'the youths', or 'the old men' as names of notes in the high treble, baritone, or bass ranges. But whatever the terminology on either side of a racial barrier, the essential musician is the same, and the qualities of musical greatness are recognizable to anyone with the gift of musical sensitivity. The Chopi composer and gifted musician stands out from his fellows in just the same way as our own virtuosi do from the common herd. 'There are those who are easily first and those who come decently after.'

Sacheverell Sitwell has recently described just such a genius as the Chopi *Timbila* leader in his account of a famous Russian xylophonist of the early nineteenth century, one Michael Joseph Gusikov.[1]

'He was a musician [he writes] in the mediaeval or oriental meaning of the word. He could not read music, and it was not necessary. Indeed, it was not written down. The music to be played was composed by instinct and instilled by ear. It would never be charged against the poets of the sagas, of the old epics, or the ballads, that they could not read or write. It was their particular poetry, and it even gained because of its special conditions or restrictions. The poems lost nothing in beauty or subtlety because they had to be got by ear. In the same way, folk music, epical or lyrical, in its hundred sorts, loses nothing because it has not the sophistication of print and paper. Rather the opposite. It loses when it is written down. Many

---

[1] Sacheverell Sitwell, *Splendours and Miseries*, Faber & Faber, 1943, p. 150 et seq.

of its nuances may be impossible to transcribe, while performance from the printed copy, in the concert hall or music room, must lack the fire and vitality of the original.'

He then goes on to describe the technique of introducing a new tune which, but for a certain romanticism in the writing, might be word for word an account of our Chopi Katini in his village near the African coast instead of the Russian Gusikov several thousand miles north.

'He takes up the hammers, and now he plays a prelude, but only to test his instrument. It is a sip or taste of the intoxicating liquor. Then comes another preluding, this time for display of speed and power, a sweep of all the notes at full force, dying away to pianissimo, so that the whole of his magical world lies open in its strangeness from end to end, as it were, from masculine to feminine in tones we have never heard before, deep and angry, but fading into enchantment. . . .

'. . . But he breaks off, suddenly, and lifts both his hammers into the air. It is the beginning. He brings down his hands together and strikes with both hammers, this time in a tremendous shake or rattle. It is the typical opening . . . it is succeeded by a pause which is indescribable in excitement while he waits again, with uplifted hands, and then beings, softly, to play one of the tunes of the Balagani.'

Would that we had our records. An introduction by Katini or Gomukomu would demonstrate just what has been described, preludes, pauses, shakes, and all, leading into the *Uetani vootsi*, the entry of the whole orchestra, as they play one of the tunes of the *Bacopi*.

But this degree of brilliance is not achieved by all, nor is it easily come by. 'To play the *Timbila* you must dream about it', is as certainly true as with any other instrument. Not only must you apply yourself to it faithfully but you must start young. No player, they told me, who took up the instrument later than his 'teens became a really good performer. For preference you should start at the age of about seven years.

A father will take his seven- or eight-year-old boy (only boys play this instrument, never girls) and sit him between his knees while he plays. The boy will hold the two beaters with his arms well flexed and pliant while the father clasps his hands over his son's and continues to play in the usual way. I asked if they ever practised scales. They said no, it was not necessary. The boy soon got to know the 'feel' of the instrument and after a few months would be able to strike any note he wanted; after a year or so he would be playing easy runs and simple variations. From then on it was a matter of daily practice and concentration. The art of highly rhythmic and harmonic playing with both hands is achieved only after years of experience. This accomplishment of theirs is so complex that European musicians almost without exception fail to grasp at first hearing what the musician is doing and how he does it. It takes us a very long while to write down even the simplest sequences, rattled off so nonchalantly by any good player.

Here is where careful recording helps our understanding. If the microphone is placed near each player in turn while he lifts one hand and continues to play with the other, you hear distinctly the intricacies of their technique, the balance of one rhythm against another or melody against contra-melody.

The zenith of a Chopi player's ambition is not to be a soloist but rather the leader of an orchestra. Before he can reach this peak he must learn to play every instrument of the orchestra, the whole gamut of devices by which each player carries out particular duties, and the limits of improvisation he is allowed at any point of the performance. There is a time when all the players must play together in unison, *kudiŋgana*, and a time when they may strike out their own variations, *kuhambana*. They must always listen for the leader's indications, *kuvelusa*, which will give warning of a change in the music, from one dance routine into another, or from dancing to singing, and so on. Should a player be engaged upon a variation of his own when he hears the *kuvelusa* he is allowed one, two, or three more repeats of the motive or measure, *indando*, in which to adjust his part to the change. Then, on the first note of the new repeat, the whole orchestra changes to whatever is required. It may be into unisons, *kuveta digando dimwedo*, as frequently happens during the singing of the lyric, or to play more loudly between verses, or to prepare for the coda. Whatever it is, the discipline of the orchestra is maintained with precision and unanimity. To hear an orchestra of twenty or more players performing with absolute assurance, improvising upon the theme or coming together in perfect unison, all without a conductor or any instructions other than their leader's *kuvelusa*, is a grand musical experience. They seem to be controlled by a sixth sense, the gift apparently enjoyed by a flock of small birds which wheel and turn with lightning rapidity in any direction yet without hesitation or indecision.

The leader of the orchestra is undoubtedly the king-pin of the whole musical structure built up in the course of a movement. His music seems to take wings and soar in a flock of notes and sequences, and he guides them with vitality and confidence from the first note to the last ringing unison upon the key-note. Father André Fernandes was right in a sense when he wrote: 'He who makes the most noise is accounted the best musician.' The fact that the leader makes his indications heard above the general sound of the orchestra, not to mention his introductions and cadenzas, would have given the old friar the impression that he was quantitatively rather than qualitatively better than the others. However good the leader, the discipline of the several and individual members of the orchestra must be perfect for him to achieve his effects.

But enough has been said to show, perhaps, that the art of a Chopi musician is far from being either primitive or simple. Whether or no the music appeals to us personally is beside the point; but that it continues to enchant the Chopi and absorb so much of their leisure is indeed important. The remarkable fertility of their composers and the intricacy of their 'ballet' removes their music from the category of mere country dances and places it upon a level of artistry well beyond that of the majority of African musicians in the southern part of the continent.

V

CHOPI MUSICIANS ON THE RAND

SEVERAL references have been made to Chopi musicians who have gone up to the wind-swept open plateau where the gold-mines of the Witwatersrand stretch out in a wide arc for a hundred and fifty miles. Along the whole periphery of this unique gold-bearing formation there rise, like man-made ant-hills of industriousness, those unmistakable landmarks which tower abruptly out of the plain and dwarf the buildings below. They are the white and grey dumps of treated sand and barren rock hauled to the surface from the deepest mines in the world. In places the rock-face of the reef is now more than 8,000 feet below the surface, and, from the moment a miner steps into the cage and leaves the daylight above him, it may take from half an hour to an hour of travelling to get to his work.

At the end of a shift you see hundreds of tired-looking natives, walking slowly, as they return to their compounds from the shaft with its rigid steel headgear and shimmering wheels. They wear the safety mining-hats which protect their heads from projecting pieces of rock, khaki shirts, trousers tied up at the knee in familiar navvy fashion, and thick boots. They carry miners' acetylene lamps and are liberally bespattered with yellow mud from the depths of the mine. They make straight for the cook-house. Here they take the rations already cooked for them, and many, there and then, sit down on the grass and eat, before going on to wash up and change their clothes. All this performed, the shift workers are themselves once again and recognizable as individuals.

Amongst this considerable army of thousands of African mine-workers, the Chopi take their place as one of the smaller of the score or more different tribes which are found on nearly every mine on the Reef. But they do more than that. Off duty they become once again Chopi, the race apart, men with the abiding passion for music and dancing.

There are over fifty Chopi orchestras of *Timbila* players and dancers on the goldfields to-day (August, 1944). It is remarkable evidence of their tribal gift for music. In the three big groups of mines alone, which are controlled from the Corner House of the Transvaal Chamber of Mines, there are forty-seven orchestras on the forty-six mines.[1] Admittedly some of the orchestras are not always up to full strength, as their members may be temporarily away back home at the coast. But out of the 6,000 or so Chopi up on the Reef at this time, no less than 780 are active musicians taking their places regularly in the weekly orchestral performances, apart from the hundreds of dancers for whom they play. This incidence of musicians must be one of the highest in the world.

For many years now they have been the show performers of the Reef compounds, and a number of the mine compound managers have taken pride in their appearances. All along the Reef you hear of competitions of dancers, guest orchestras, and gala performances for some visiting celebrity or other. I must make special mention of one compound manager in particular, Mr. L. G. Hallett of the C.M.R. (Consolidated Main Reef Mines and Estates, Ltd.). Mr. Hallett has a reputation for taking a great interest in all the various artistic activities of the native miners under his charge. Recently he completed a dance arena of semicircular design constructed in stone, for the express purpose of providing a suitable place for dancing displays. It is reminiscent of a Roman amphitheatre and holds about 2,500 spectators. Mr. Hallett had already made a square dance-floor at another of the mines where he was previously engaged, but I persuaded him to adopt the semicircular design as more suitable for the purpose. The result has amply justified his industry, and the Chopi musicians of his compounds as well as the dancers of a dozen other tribes are delighted at the recognition by their employers of their inherent talents. One Chopi I asked said, with obvious satisfaction, he thought this dance arena 'very up to date'.

I have not been able to make a complete survey of the orchestras in the mine compounds, but I visited several within a dozen miles

[1] See List of Chopi Orchestras in Appendix III.

of the city. There I had conversations with many of the *wasiki watimbila*, the orchestra leaders, some of whom I had previously met in their own villages in Zavala. They confirmed the impressions I had gathered from their friends and relatives at home, and indicated a state of affairs in the Chopi musical world along the Reef which I now describe.

As one would expect, there are not enough good leaders and composers of the first rank to lead all the mine orchestras. Consequently there are many men who are rated second and third in their home orchestras leading *Ŋgodo* in the Transvaal. On the other hand, there are said to be at least half a dozen really good men on the Reef to-day who are both leaders and composers of note. Among them I was specially recommended to Twelfu, from Galiondo's village, Mandhlagazi, Chidengele district, at the Simmer and Jack mine; Dochikane Nyantombo of Mwene's village in the same district, at the C.M.R. mine; Machipisi and the blind Chipendani, both from Kanda's village, Zavala district, who led the orchestras at the Langlaagte and East Geduld mines respectively. There must be many others of equal calibre whose names were not given me.

These men, original composers, have little difficulty in providing new and topical material for their performances. I asked some of them if it was true that music composed away from home was not so good as their home compositions. They replied that they could make up the music all right away from home, but life was dull at the mines in comparison with their villages and so there were fewer incidents upon which to hang their poetry. Without their women and children and the social round of the seasons this is easily appreciated. Their poetry, you will have noticed, is objective and topical, and one would not expect the Chopi to decline into the drawing-room ballad and expatiate upon the glory of the sunset or the miracle of a tree. Subject-matter, therefore, is limited, and what new material is found seems to deal with mine life, the petty tyrannies of overseers, the eternal taxes, and such-like thorns in the flesh. Unfortunately I have not yet had the opportunity of taking down in full any *Ŋgodo* produced exclusively on the mines, and so, for the time being, we can only guess their contents. What I have found so far is a conglomerate of village compositions borrowed from a dozen villages and put together almost at random to make up the eleven movements of the *Ŋgodo*. Twelfu, of the Simmer and Jack mine, had taken one of Gomukomu's *Msitso* for his new *Ŋgodo*. I recognized the tune and asked him about it. He admitted it was not his own composition, but he liked it, and one of his players, who had recently come up from Filippe Banguza's kraal, had taught it to the rest of the orchestra. I found several of Katini's compositions at other compounds. They appeared to be quite *au fait* with the latest work of their better-known composers. Blande Zavala, for example, younger brother of the Paramount Chief Wani Zavala, who has been away from home for ten years or more, was fully acquainted with the poetry of Katini's last (1943) *Ŋgodo* which his men were now performing at the Village Main mine, though Katini himself had not visited the Reef.

The players of the mine orchestras, unlike those of the village orchestras, are not all drawn from the same district. Individual players have certain loyalties to particular mines to which they return again and again. Then once on the Reef, they play with whatever musicians happen to be up with them. In this way the music of the Chopi has become common national music and no longer exclusively village or district music. It is a development which brings both advantages and disadvantages in its train.

The advantages are obvious. Their national music has a chance of becoming widely known, and individuals find a far wider range of composers through whom they may obtain their musical satisfaction. Musicians widen their repertoire and dancers their routines to an extent which would have been unlikely if not impossible had they stayed at home in their villages. All this is good for the development of a national music and consequently for the social satisfactions to be derived from it. But there are mechanical disadvantages.

The first and foremost of these problems is the one of tonality, a common scale and a common pitch. As we shall see, there is not yet agreement upon these points in the villages, and the most eminent composers and leaders cannot bring themselves to forgo their local idiosyncrasies. Yet when they play on the mines, they must willy nilly accept the local tuning and play accordingly. Clearly, therefore, a solution can be found if sufficient pressure be brought to bear to make it worth while to conform. This is fundamentally a problem for the instrument-makers. If a maker or makers could be persuaded to undertake the manu-

PLATE XIII

a. Bulafu weMpambanisa, Timbila maker to the village of Zandamela, who altered his tuning to that of Katini at Zavala's village. This excellent old musician suffers from eye trouble and is no longer able to make his instruments as he used to do, but his ear is as good as ever

b. Muchini Ndambuzi, Leader of the Orchestra at the village of Chief Davida, demonstrates the method of playing Timbila while standing or walking with the arc of the instrument keeping it away from his body and the band, *Likhole kupakata*, slung round his neck bearing the weight

PLATE XIV

a. Detail of a Timbila with round arc, showing the membrane vibrators inside their protecting 'trumpets', some of which are cracked and need replacing. The lower side of the tips of some of the notes, it will be seen, have been pared away to raise the pitch when tuning

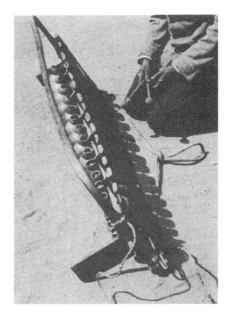

b. The Malimba Xylophones of the Shangana-Ndau. The musician, Whoseni Pedro Tunzini, lost the use of his legs in an accident in the gold mines and now devotes himself to his music. The three instruments are called *Sekanajo*, the Accompaniment (the top one), *Munyekera*, the Leader (the centre one), and *Gulu*, the Bass (the lower one). Between them they cover a range of three and a half octaves. The drums are also played in threes under the names of the Great, the Small, and the Middle drum—*Ŋgomahuru*, *Ŋgomadoko*, and *Ŋgomayepagati*. The xylophones have no legs like those of the Chopi, and the resonators are protected by a strip of hide stretched tightly under them and attached to the backbone of the instrument

facture of a standard *Timbila* tuned to a standard scale and pitch for the Reef compounds, it would greatly enhance the pleasure of the musicians by enabling them to play in any orchestra or, for special occasions, to combine any two or more orchestras in mass performances. At present, on such occasions as the visit of the Portuguese President already mentioned, the effect of combining local orchestras is, to say the least, somewhat disappointing.

The quality of the instruments played on the Reef is not good, and this is entirely due to the lack of proper materials. Although, through the generosity of many mine managers, wood and other materials have been provided and Chopi instrument-makers detailed to devote some of their time to this work, the results have been inferior in every way to the home-made product. Some managers have encouraged musicians to bring back supplies from Portuguese East Africa, but there again trouble with the authorities, railways and customs, generally results, they say, in their losing their precious materials *en route*.

The poor quality can be traced directly to the use of light wood for the notes and straight-sided tins for resonators. Since the shape of the resonating body is a material factor in the production of good tone, this substitution makes for poor tone. Some of the orchestras I have heard on the Reef have better tone than others, but I fully agree with the Chopi who claim that none of the Reef orchestras sound so good as the fine *Mwenje* wood instruments of their homes. It is a situation which should be remedied.

Musicians would gladly bring instruments with them from Zavala were it not for the expense incurred and the risk of having them confiscated at the border. One mine compound manager told me that he had great difficulty in persuading the customs authorities on the border to part with a confiscated instrument which he had specially requested one of his musicians to bring up with him. The cost of transporting *Timbila* is far too expensive for native purses. The *Timbila* are classed as musical instruments by the railway officials and have to be paid for at the same rates as expensive European instruments of a hundred times their value. Thus the rate on a *Timbila*, which a Chopi is not allowed to carry as personal luggage, is generally considerably more than the cost of the instrument itself. No wonder the Chopi are forced to leave their instruments behind and put up with the poor-quality *Timbila* provided for them on the mines.

The same ban does not appear to operate with regard to the accoutrements worn by the dancers. A surprisingly large number of them bring their jackal-skin capes, *didowo*, their yellow dancing-cloth, *ŋguwo*, and their angora-goat leggings, *diwaka*. From what I have seen they appear to dance as well as they do at home, but I understand they are inclined to stick to simpler routines on account of the fact that they are drawn from many different villages and they have to learn new steps to fit in with the others. Leadership with the dancers is also a question, and good dance-leaders, like good orchestral leaders, are not always available in all the compounds.

Little more is known about Chopi musicians away from their homes, as virtually no one has either written or recorded their music satisfactorily. Half a dozen records, mostly of poor quality, is all the evidence we have of this outstanding African music. I have made about twenty acetate records so far, but we shall have to wait a short while longer until more normal times before we can make master-records to be published commercially.

Reference is often made on the Reef to the playing of certain European melodies on *Timbila* by Chopi musicians. It is taken by unmusical Europeans as a sign of musical promise. In point of fact, it is nothing of the sort. I have heard many of these tunes, such as 'Tea for Two', 'Sarie Marais', and so on. They play them very simply in unison, with the right hand, with an occasional blow upon the tonic with the left. They have learnt to play these tunes, grossly out of tune upon their whole-tone scale, as a gesture of courtesy to the white people. 'God save the King' or the Portuguese National Anthem is also played, often immediately preceding the Orchestral Finale of the *Ŋgodo*. All are very simple affairs in comparison with even the most elementary movements of their own music. They demonstrate with the utmost clarity that the attempt to mix artistic media is nearly always a failure and musically frightful. That the Chopi are encouraged in this by some Europeans is childish on our part, and that they comply is but a child-like compliment on theirs.

We can now see with reasonable certainty that the Chopi are capable of advanced musical achievement; and, by the manner in which villagers from all parts of the country co-operate with all comers to keep up their art though away from home, that they are nearer, perhaps, than any other tribe in southern Africa to creating a national music out of their several, but geographically circumscribed, village musics. What they need on the mines, as well as in their own villages, is further support from well-informed persons. Their music and dancing have already assured them of the popular support of other Africans in the compounds and the occasional patronage of white tourists, employers, and casual philanthropists. Detailed knowledge of their music, poetry, and songs should help to direct the potential flow of support into more fruitful channels.

Chopi musicians merit a reputation far beyond their own borders, and, with the coming of recording apparatus, this may not be long delayed, even though they never leave their familiar woods and lakes in Portuguese East Africa.

And after all has been told about them, we who follow in the steps of Father André Fernandes cannot but agree with him when he described them as 'these fortunate people', with their great capacity for music; after four centuries, it is still as he said: 'They are much given to the pleasures of singing and playing.'

As a direct result of my measuring their scales and drawing their attention to the desirability of a common pitch, the leaders of the four main orchestras in Zavala have now voluntarily adopted the same pitch (H. T., 1947).

For a list of published records of *timbila* music see Appendix IV, p. 164.

VI

TIMBILA, THE XYLOPHONES OF THE CHOPI

Description of the Instrument

THE *Timbila* of the Chopi are perhaps the most interesting of the musical instruments of the southern Bantu. The small 'hand-pianos', the *Mbira* of the Zambesi valley for which the Portuguese have the delightful name of 'Pianino', are the only instruments comparable in range and musicality, and nowadays the *Mbira* are not so frequently played in ensembles. The Chopi *Ŋgodo* with its full orchestra and dancers is almost unique.

The history and distribution of the xylophone in Africa is fairly well known. It can be traced all the way from the Chopi country in the south-east at Cape Corrientes across Africa in two sweeps, the southern ending in the Congo and the northern in west Africa. From the scanty evidence available at present it seems that, of all the tribes using xylophones, only a minority have a heptatonic scale. The remainder use a hexatonic, pentatonic, or even smaller scale. So it seems permissible to suggest at this stage that the Chopi instrument is as good as, if not better than, the majority of its kind on this continent. It is excellently made by skilled craftsmen, though perhaps not quite so neat as the *Malimba* xylophones to be found two hundred miles farther north on the coast near the great Sabi river, where they are played by the Shangana-Ndau people. These two, the *Timbila* and the *Malimba*, are the only xylophones found on the east coast of Africa, if we are to accept our present authorities, more particularly Olga Boone of the Musée du Congo Belge.

The appearance of the *Marimba* in South America is therefore easily explained when we remember that the first of many boat-loads of African slaves was known to have been taken from this coast to Brazil about the year 1530.

The instrument has been described briefly by writers on the Chopi and neighbouring tribes, beginning with Father André Fernandes. Most of them have given general descriptions which are accurate as far as they go, and I shall attempt to add to the sum of their evidence by describing the instruments I have examined during the past four years.

The Chopi xylophones, *Timbila*, are made primarily to be played in ensembles and not for solo work, although naturally, individual musicians are found playing by themselves, and a solo instrument is said to accompany *Ŋgalaŋga*, children's dances with drums. The music is composed essentially to be played by a number of instruments, and it is in this combination that the *Timbila* is heard to best effect. Several musicians have told me that they only played the tunes from the various *Migodo* and had no other solo pieces in their repertoire.

There are five kinds of *Timbila* manufactured and played by the present-day Chopi which may be broadly classified by their equivalent English names: Treble, *Cilanzane* or *Malanzane*; Alto, *Saŋge* or *Sanje*; Tenor, *Dole* or *Mbiŋgwe*; Bass, *Debiinda*; and Double Bass, *Gulu* or *Kulu*. Each of these instruments has its own function to perform in the orchestra, but to-day the tenor instrument, *Dole*, is not often found. They say it is not so easy to play, for its range lies between the easier parts of *Saŋge* and *Debiinda*. At the same time they all regret that there are not more *Dole* to be found. Both Katini and Gomukomu assured me that you must have at least one *Dole* in an orchestra, if you can find the man to play it, to get a well-balanced performance.

With the exception of the double bass, *Gulu*, all the instruments overlap each other in range. Between them they cover just over four octaves. The treble xylophone, *Cilanzane*, invariably starts from the key-note called *Hombe* and has from twelve to sixteen notes. The alto xylophone, *Saŋge*, has one, two, or three additional notes below *Hombe*, and may have from fourteen to eighteen notes. The tenor xylophone, *Dole*, as a rule starts from the note four or five below *Hombe* and may have ten to fourteen notes. The bass xylophone, *Debiinda*, starts an octave below *Hombe* and usually has ten notes. The double bass, *Gulu*, has three or four notes which are not always tuned the same. Katini maintains that they should always be tuned to two octaves below *Hombe* with the other three or four notes corresponding to notes

Nos. 2, 3, and 5. But variations of this rule are found with notes still deeper.

DIAGRAM III. *Showing the normal range and distribution of notes in a Chopi orchestra*

	Number		Name of note and range	*Cilanzane*	*Sange*	*Dole*	*Debiinda*	*Gulu*
	16		*digumi nidimwedo*	×	×			
Octave″	15		*digumi nicanu*	×	×			
	14		*digumi nimune*	×	×			
	13		*digumi nimararu*	×	×			
	12		*digumi nimambidi*	×	×			
	11		*digumi dimwedo*	×	×			
	10		*digumi*	×	×			
	9		*nimune*	×	×			
Octave′	8	*Hombe idoko*	*nimararu*	×	×			
	7		*nimambidi* CILANZANE	×	×	×		
	6		*nedimwedu*	×	×	×		
	5		*canu*	×	×	×		
	4		*mune*	×	×	×		
	3		*mararu*	×	×	×	×	
	2		*mambidi*	×	×	×	×	
Tonic	1	HOMBE	*dimwedo*	×	×	×	×	
	3		*mararu*		×	×	×	
	2		*mambidi* SAŊGE		×	×	×	
	1		*dimwedo*		×	×	×	
	4		*mune*		(×)	×	×	
	3		*mararu*			×	×	
	2		*mambidi* DEBIINDA				×	
,Octave,	1	(*Hombe*)	*dimwedo*				×	
	—		—					
	—		—					
	4		*mune*					×
	—		—					
	3		*mararu* GULU					×
	2		*mambidi*					×
,,Octave,,	1	(*Hombe*)	*dimwedo*					×

There are sometimes one or two additional notes both in the treble (Nos. 17 and 18) and below the lowest note shown in the bass.

All the notes are referred to by numbers starting from *Hombe*, and no note, except *Hombe* and its octaves, has a name other than its numeral. The outside notes on an instrument may be called 'the end right', *magumo kanyamboswe*, i.e. the top note in the treble, or 'the end left', *magumo manyadye*, the bottom note in the bass; but these refer to the two outside notes on any instrument whatever the pitch may be. The notes themselves are called after the instrument in the range of which they lie, with apparently the exception of *Dole*. The diagram of the range of the *Timbila* orchestra makes this clearer (Diagram III).

It can be assumed that, apart from the one name *Hombe*, and possibly *Hombe idoko*, none of the notes is named for its musical pitch but for its relative position on the instrument.[1] The wooden slat, before it is fixed into an instrument, is called *dikokoma* (pl. *makokoma*); once it is fixed into position in the instrument it becomes a note of the instrument *mbila* (pl. *timbila*) emitting a musical sound or note, *dipṣui* (pl. *mapṣui*).

Timbila may be described as resonated xylophones, tuned to perform in orchestras of any number of players from five to thirty or more. The most popular instrument is the *Saŋge*, which is found in greater numbers than the others. The leader of the orchestra, *musiki watimbila*, usually plays a *Saŋge*. The virtuosity of his playing, particularly in the solo cadenzas, demands an instrument of wide range. In well-made instruments the tonality is good in all ranges of pitch, though in common with instrument makers the world over, Chopi makers find difficulty in cutting and tuning the deeper notes, particularly those of the *Gulu*.

The scales used by Chopi musicians are not yet fully known, but the evidence so far leads us towards certain conclusions which will now be discussed.

The Tuning of Timbila

Our knowledge of the scales used by Chopi musicians and the tuning by which they achieve them has previously been very much a matter of guess-work. This has been due to the absence of any adequate means of measurement. The human ear is notoriously accommodating and, unaided by fixed physical norms, is liable to lend itself to grave errors at the whim or prejudice of the mind behind it. So the field has been anyone's ground who cared to express an opinion. Even with reasonably exact

---

[1] P. R. Kirby (*Musical Instruments of the Native Races of South Africa*, Oxford, 1934) gives the names of notes supplied by one informant. I have not been able to confirm this elsewhere, so it may be a personal or local idiosyncrasy, confined to one group or district.

equipment for measuring the pitch it is easy to be mistaken or to give an interpretation to a sound which is not shared by the native musician. I have measured several hundred instruments by means of a set of tuning-forks. My forks are tuned from 212 vibrations per second up to the octave 424 vibrations, one fork to each division of four vibrations. With this set of fifty-four forks I have been enabled to determine the pitch of notes to within plus or minus two vibrations, which should be accurate enough for general research purposes.

When measuring the notes I invariably enlist the aid of the native musician in choosing the right tuning-fork to correspond with his note. I have always been impressed by the accuracy with which they determine the exact fork, which shows at least a sense of discrimination. Any suggestion that the scales of instruments such as the *Timbila* are purely arbitrary and assembled by mere chance must be rejected from the evidence already collected. There are areas in southern Africa where I cannot trace any sign of agreement between musicians in the tuning of their instruments; the south-eastern corner of Southern Rhodesia is one, where the Ndau appear to have only a rudimentary sense of the fitness of their hexatonic scales and not only fail to tune the octave correctly but disagree so widely among themselves that no two *Mbira* instruments can be played together with comfort. But this is unusual, and, in nearly every area which shows a relatively undisturbed history, the similarity of tuning among the tribe's musicians is more remarkable than are the dissimilarities. Beyond this statement we are not yet in a position to go, until further work has been undertaken and the general opinion of native musicians has been studied. However, with Chopi musicians, who are by far the most musically developed in southern Africa, the solution of the problem is much nearer. They have had a relatively undisturbed history since they arrived on the coast from the highlands of Monomotapa in the late fifteenth or early sixteenth century. Inter-breeding between tribes does not appear to have affected the Chopi very much as they are a proud people, living aloof and apart from neighbours in adjacent districts upon whom they look down. The Ndau, on the other hand, were recently, within the century, conquered by the Shangaans and have a considerable sprinkling of Shangaan blood in their veins. To what extent this genetic factor influences the tuning of musical instruments where no physical standard in the scientific sense is available yet remains to be seen. What indications there are at present appear to point towards a psycho-physical norm which leads the closely related members of any tribe to prefer certain similar musical intervals in their scales, and in some cases to achieve an agreement in the pitch of the tonic which, to us, to say the least, is remarkable. Although environment and youthful impressions may be largely responsible for our musical taste in after years, it seems likely that those impressions are seasoned by something deeper than the experiences of one's own lifetime alone.

Musical ability, they say, is a Mendelian dominant, and when discussing the music of a tribe we are, in fact, referring to the propensities of the musical members of that tribe. To what extent blood-grouping influences the inherent choice of the musical intervals of a scale remains to be seen. I have found that the average tuning of the Chopi orchestras in Zavala is almost identical with the average tuning of the *Njari*, the hand-piano or *pianino*, of the Karanga people of Southern Rhodesia from whom they separated 450 years ago but whose blood-grouping has remained almost the same.[1]

Tuning in cents (100 cents = 1 tempered semitone)

| Karanga | 0 | 176 | 346 | 519 | 675 | 853 | 1,032 | 1,200 |
| Chopi | 0 | 176 | 345 | 519 | 680 | 854 | 1,029 | 1,200 |

Whenever I have measured their scales I have asked the musicians concerned to try to explain to me the foundation of their musical preferences. On 26 September, 1943, having previously noted down most of the scales mentioned in this work, I held a conference of leading Chopi musicians and instrument makers at Quissico, in the Zavala district, their home in Moçambique. The meeting was attended by four *Timbila* makers, *muwati watimbila*, Katini weNyamombe of Zavala's kraal, Bulafu weMpambanisa of Zandamela's kraal, Majanyana weMoyeni of Banguza's kraal, and Jumbosi weSamboko of Jambula's kraal; in addition to these, there were four orchestra leaders, *musiki watimbila*, as well as Katini who is the senior musician of the country and is both maker and leader: Nyampose weNyarizeze,

[1] Ronald Elsdon Dew, M.D., *Blood Groups in Africa*, published by the South African Institute of Medical Research, No. XLIV, vol. x, pp. 29–94 (1939).

the blind leader of Nyakutowo's kraal, Sauli Ilova waMahika of Mavila's kraal, Tawani wePandhlani of Mugande's kraal, and Sipingani weLikwekwe of Chisiko's kraal. These men between them, with certain notable absentees, represent the best and most musically informed opinion of the tribe. The glossary of musical terms[1] was checked in their presence and agreed upon. Any inadequacies found must be laid at the door of faulty interpretation or misunderstanding. Their opinions therefore must have considerable weight and be more reliable than individual opinions expressed by various musicians while away from home on the Rand mines.

For four hours we sat and discussed musical terminology and lore. It was most enlightening to hear them argue as to which was the most correct pitch for the tone centre, *Hombe*. Katini maintained that, as the Paramount Chief's musician, his was the one and only correct pitch, his was the 'king's note', vouchsafed to him by his father, grandfather, and ancestors who had been hereditary leaders and composers of the king's music for generations. He may be right. No one can bring a better case. The other musicians had equally good claims to hold the norm, but they were based upon the patronage of somewhat lesser chiefs. Bulafu of Zandamela, whom I met first in 1940 and again in 1941, admitted to being converted to Katini's tuning after I had pointed out to him the divergence in the pitch of their two instruments. He lives at the other end of the district and had not come in contact with Katini very much. But when he discovered for himself the truth of what I told him, he dropped his pitch a whole minor tone to that of Katini's. When I returned in 1943 I noticed the change and he told me what he had done.

But in spite of a divergence of opinion as to the exact and desirable pitch of the Tonic, they all agreed that each in his own way was attempting to achieve the same kind of scale, an even scale of seven intervals, all alike. The proof of their several and separate successes in achieving this end is strikingly substantiated in the measurements I had already taken and now show in diagrammatic form (Diagrams IV and V). When one remembers the difference of opinion on this very point of pitch and equal temperament which raged in Europe up to the middle of the last century (and to some extent still rages), it is remarkable how

[1] See Appendix II.

far the Chopi have progressed with no substantial criteria other than their musical integrity. It is clear they owe nothing to any foreign contact or teaching, either in the construction of their instruments or in their compositions.

DIAGRAM IV. *Showing the tuning of five orchestras in the Zavala District*

(*Note*: Zandamela has since retuned to that of Zavala with Hombe 252)

(*a*) *In vibrations per second*

	Zavala	Chisiko	Mavila	Banguza	Zandamela
Octave	504	512	520	520	552
	456	472	464	472	496
	408	424	424	432	448
	368	384	384	388	408
	336	348	352	356	368
	304	316	320	316	336
	276	288	284	288	308
Hombe	252	256	260	260	276

(*b*) *In cents* (100 *cents* = 1 *tempered semitone*)

	Zavala		Chisiko		Mavila		Banguza		Zandamela		Average	
Octave	1,200		1,200		1,200		1,200		1,200		1,200	
		173		141		197		168		184		173
	1,027		1,059		1,003		1,032		1,016		1,027	
		193		185		173		153		177		176
	834		874		830		879		839		851	
		179		172		155		186		162		171
	655		702		675		693		677		680	
		157		170		150		149		179		161
	498		532		525		544		498		519	
		173		168		166		207		157		174
	325		364		359		337		341		345	
		168		160		206		160		151		169
	157		204		153		177		190		176	
		157		204		153		177		190		176
Hombe	0		0		0		0		0		0	

Owing to mathematical difficulties, it is essential to reduce all intervals measured in vibrations per second to a common norm in relationship to our tempered scale. The method devised by A. J. Ellis in 1885[1] is the one used here. It reduces all intervals

[1] 'The Musical Scales of Various Nations', by A. J. Ellis, in the *Journal of the Society of Arts* for March 1885, London. Quoted by Joseph Yasser in his book, *A Theory of Evolving Tonality*, American Library of Musicology.

proportionally to the tempered semitone which is given the value of 100 cents. The octave is therefore 1,200 cents. By this method the values of the Just and the Tempered Scales can be readily calculated and a fair comparison can be made between all musical scales and ratios.

If you study these figures you will notice that the pitch of the Tonic *Hombe* only varies eight vibrations if the tuning of Zandamela is discounted since they have voluntarily changed to that of Zavala. This means that the difference of opinion amongst the leading Chopi musicians is no more than that between European musicians of the last century. The wider divergence found outside the borders of their home country must be accounted for by the ignorance of those manufacturers who, they tell me, are often only semi-skilled and not approved craftsmen. There may yet be found a more exact reason for the discrepancy, but this would seem to be an adequate one. It was amusing to listen to their earnest and indeed somewhat heated arguments in defence of their own pitch for *Hombe*. It has taken us centuries to achieve a standard for ourselves, and as Percy Scholes says,[1] 'the existence of a universally accepted standard of pitch (amongst Europeans) must, by any who have traced the fluctuations, be regarded as a triumph of human co-operation'. What fluctuations there may still be amongst the Chopi remain to be seen. In the old days, and up till now, there was little urgency to come to some standard agreement upon the pitch of instruments. Villages were far apart and musicians played mostly with their own folk. There were times, they said, when they found it inconvenient to be out of tune when they went visiting another district and could not take part without having to retune their instruments. Katini, although most conservative on the point, volunteered to retune his own instrument when he visited Durban with me, as the other five musicians had the pitch of Banguza's village, eight vibrations higher, *Hombe* 260. When he returned home he retuned his instrument to his own pitch. Some of the musicians not of his village whom he took to Lisbon with him on his two visits to Europe for exhibitions in Portugal, the second for the Centenary celebrations in 1940, were similarly forced to accept *his* tuning.

But on special occasions, like the famous one mentioned in his

[1] *Oxford Companion to Music*, Oxford, p. 732.

songs when the President visited the colony, all the Chopi musicians from the whole country-side were called upon to go and play. They say that at Magul they did not tune up to one pitch as it was only for a single day and the work involved was considerable. I can imagine the noise that must have issued from the massed orchestra! Yet the excitement and pomp of the moment must have overshadowed this shortcoming, which, after all, would probably not have been noticed by the *Mwama Ŋkulu*, the President, who was unacquainted with their music, nor indeed by any of the Europeans present.

Although this occasional lapse into, or tolerance of, out-of-tuneness occurs, it is admitted and regretted by the strict musicians and would not be allowed by leaders such as Katini or Gomukomu in their own orchestras. I was present one day at a performance by Chopi musicians at the small village of Manhiça on the high bank of the Incomati river. They had been called by the Administrador of the district to come and play for me. This small isolated group of Chopi under Chief Davida have settled in the Manhiça district, having left their home country in search of work in this fertile valley. Among them was an old musician who had recently come down from Zavala to live with his relatives and had brought his *Timbila* with him. It was hopelessly out of tune with the others and he had not the skill to retune it, but he played with them nevertheless. When I asked the leader Muchini Ndambuzi why he tolerated an instrument so much out of tune he replied, 'Well, the old man is very fond of music.' He had not the heart to ask him either to stop playing or to retune his instrument. Katini or Bulafu would have done the job for him without delay.

With the opening up of the country and the greater mobility of the native peoples unimpeded by hostile neighbours, the question of the proper pitch of their *Timbila* must inevitably become more pressing, if only on account of the large number of orchestras along the Reef. What the final choice will be, should an accepted standard of pitch be adopted, one cannot say, but the claim of the Paramount Chief's musician Katini to *Hombe* 252 cannot, for historic and political reasons, be overlooked.

We can safely accept the assurances of the home musicians that, whatever the pitch of the Tonic, they are all in their own way attempting to achieve an even scale of equal intervals, a kind of tempered heptatonic scale. If we can establish such a scale for them scientifically and provide a standard norm in the form of suitable tuning-forks or bars, the chances are well in favour of its acceptance by the majority of musicians who wish to be able to play in more than one orchestra, and it might well be introduced on the Rand.

But it is not only the pitch of the Tonic which is in doubt. Some of them still cling to the inclusion of perfect fourth or perfect fifth in the scale. This is impossible in a well-tempered whole minor tone heptatonic scale, which requires the fourth to be considerably sharpened and the fifth flattened. Katini's scale includes the fourth and Gomukomu's the fifth, but neither have both. Personally (and it will be noted that the opinion of Europeans is of little account in this matter), I have developed a preference for Gomukomu's scale over Katini's, which to me is a little dull with his severely flattened fifth. But this one would expect from a European background. The matter must ultimately be given a fair trial and be judged upon its merits by a tribunal of the leading musicians of the tribe. The advantages would, I expect, be understood and enjoyed by musicians who have the opportunity of travelling farther afield than their own village. Much more investigation will be necessary before we can justifiably suggest a solution.

As for the musicians away at work, we must assume that they will follow their acknowledged leaders at home. Every Chopi readily admits that the home music is best. The instruments on the Rand are known to be in most cases poor substitutes for the full-tone *Timbila* from the woods of Zavala, and the *Migodo* sung in the locations are but echoes of the real music shimmering through the great shade-trees of home. 'How can we sing the songs of Zion in a strange land?'

Once we have given them the lead and published the whole case of Chopi music with clarity and understanding, my impression is that they will seize the opportunity of smoothing out discrepancies and faults, of which all their sensitive musicians are well aware, and will establish the art on a still more secure foundation. Our scientific contribution is, indeed, all that we can make and all that is necessary. Regular publication of their poetry and music, either in book form or on gramophone records, will give them both the criteria and the status necessary to establish their art and confirm their reputation. We must not look upon Chopi music from the point of view of its concert-platform value in the future, but rather from that of its practical and social value in the present, and that means at home in the villages and abroad in the locations. The study of the tuning of their instruments may reveal a practical norm and sweep aside many of the handicaps which they already deplore and which only their lack of science maintains.

The Manufacture of Timbila

Like many other country crafts, the manufacture of musical instruments is often found in families, the art being handed down from father to son. This seems to be the case with the manufacture of the *Timbila*. It is not exclusively in the hands of these families, but the skill and feeling for the work appear to be more developed in the sons of craftsmen. A comparatively few men in the tribe are responsible for all the instruments used. I have not a complete list of *Timbila* makers, *wavati watimbila*, but from what they say, not every orchestra has its own maker, and those villages without one have to rely on the services of their neighbours. And not every maker is a good craftsman. It is easy to discern varying degrees of skill in the manufacture of the instruments. In Zavala and Banguza's villages the instruments show particularly high craftsmanship. At Zavala nearly all the instruments were made by Katini and his son Katinyana. At Banguza most of them were made by Majanyana's father, who died only a few years ago, and now his two sons have taken up the craft.

Repairs can be effected by nearly every musician, but the actual manufacture is left to those who specialize in it. I will try to describe in detail the work and knowledge which is required on the part of a Chopi craftsman to turn out a well-tuned instrument.

The materials required for the making of a *Timbila* are all found in the country-side around their villages. They are these:

Mukusu	wood for the main frame of the instrument.
Mwenje	wood for the wooden slats which make the notes.
Matamba	'gourds', the hard shell of a wild fruit for the resonators and trumpets of the smaller notes, field gourds for the larger.

Ipula	bees-wax of the ground bee.
Iŋgoti	bark string or thongs of hide for supporting the notes.
Mbuŋgo	rubber for the rubber-headed beaters.
Ivondo (ya kwewa)	the diaphragm of the jerboa, or the peritoneum of cattle for the reverberating membrane.

The tools required are very simple:

Njiwatelo	a small sharp adze.
Mbato	a home-made chisel.
Ntombo	a metal spike for burning holes.
Ŋgwaruto or *peniheni*	a small wooden tool for working the wax (Fig. X)

and the usual axe *nzaŋga* for cutting down trees, a knife *ciwatelo* for shaping and carving patterns, a rib-bone for polishing the notes, *mbalahuta* leaves, which act as sandpaper, and a scraper of metal or broken glass, *dibono*. With this simple equipment the Chopi *Timbila* maker will produce a beautiful and musically perfect instrument (see Diagrams VI and VII, p. 136).

Now assuming that all the materials are collected together, which in practice would not be the case as they would mostly be fetched as the work went on, we will follow the maker in his work of constructing a *Timbila*. First he makes the frame of the *Timbila*. In doing so he uses no measurements at all but appears to work by eye, with the keen sense of the fitness of shape which their age-old craft has taught them. By this ingrained sense he tapers his wood where it needs tapering and guesses the gradually diminishing distances needed to set his notes in perfect line, each distance carefully set off to preserve a kind of balance.

First he makes the backbone of the instrument, *mugwama* (Fig. III), of *mukusu* wood, the Mafureira Nut tree (*Trichilia emetica*). This stout board is slightly tapered towards the treble and at each end he carves out two tenons, *dinsoŋgola*, which are to fit into two holes in the legs of the instrument and into the ends of the arc. He now marks out the positions of the holes, *matsoko*, to be cut through the backbone; each hole will lie directly below its note and on the lower side it will lead to the resonator. The holes are now cut about an inch in diameter by using the small chisel and are finished off with the knife. Now two small holes are burnt, by means of a small metal spike, *ntombo*, diagonally into each of the holes from the lower side. These holes are for the purpose of fixing the resonators firmly to the backbone by tying them on with bark string, *ŋgoti*. The *mugwama* is now completed.

Next, he fixes the resonating gourds on to the backbone. He will have made a large collection of the hard-shelled fruit *matamba* of the *nsala* or *mtamba*, Kaffir Orange tree (*Strychnos spinosa*). He removes the pips and soft pulp through a clean-cut circular hole at the top of the fruit where it is attached to the stem. He carefully grades the fruits into sizes from small shells about $1\frac{1}{2}$ inches diameter only, to resonate the highest notes, down to shells 4 to 6 inches diameter. For the lowest notes of *Debiinda*, the bass *Timbila*, he will most likely be unable to find *matamba* large enough and will have to resort to gourds from the fields. The resonators for *Gulu*, the double-bass *Timbila*, will need to be outsize gourds at that, 14 to 16 inches deep. The explanation behind this is the simple one which applies to all musical instruments; the smaller the vibrating material, whether it be solid or gaseous, the smaller or higher the note produced. It can also be explained in terms of the wave-lengths of the pitch of musical notes which get shorter with the ascending scale. When he collects *matamba* he brings back a good many more than he requires, to allow for breakages and spares. These must be dried in the sun before they are used.

Having selected his resonators, he drills two holes in each, near the mouth. Through these he threads the string, *kusuŋga kuŋgoti*, which will then be passed through the corresponding holes already bored in the backbone (Fig. VII), and the resonator will then be tied firmly on. The joint is made airtight with *ipula* wax. This is a black wax from the ground bees, *ipembe*, and its full name is *ipula ya pembe*. In its natural state the wax is inclined to be too hard and is softened by adding the poisonous oil expressed from the fruit of the Mafureira[1] tree. This *ipula* is an essential ingredient in the art of *Timbila* making, for all joints must be airtight or the notes will not reverberate properly.

---

[1] *Trichilia emetica*, Malfura or Mafureira nut (Meliaciae). A handsome East African deciduous tree, yielding 60–80 lb. dry nuts per tree. Nuts rich in fatty oil, edible, and used in the manufacture of soaps and candles. The residue of the seeds is considered poisonous (*Tropical Planting and Gardening*, by A. F. MacMillan, p. 381).

The two legs of the instrument are the next to be made. These are called *nenje* (pl. *minenje*) or sometimes *nenge* (pl. *minenge*). The legs are about 9 inches tall by 4 inches across, in the case of the *Cilanzane* or *Sange*, and slightly taller for *Dole* and *Debiinda* in order to ensure that the resonating gourds clear the ground. The legs of the double bass, *Gulu*, are from 30 to 36 inches tall as this instrument is played standing. They are sometimes solid and sometimes carved into the shape of two legs with a foot, *mkondo*. The design of the leg amongst other things is the hall-mark of the various makers. Near the top of the legs two holes are bored to fit over the tenons on the ends of the backbone. Some legs are even mortised to fit more snugly into the backbone.

The next job is to make the straining bars and distance pieces which support the weight of the notes. The straining bars, *murari kutsanisa timbila* (Fig. IV), are made as a rule in one piece out of *mukusu* wood. This forms an arc round the instrument whose function is threefold: to prevent the instrument from falling right over when on the ground, to assist the player in his control of the instrument while he plays (many players by twisting their leg over this arc occasionally lift their instrument off the ground and play with it swaying in the air), and to act as a distance piece to keep the instrument away from the body when it is played while standing or walking. This arc is sometimes made up in three pieces with the corners squared. This fashion appears to be due to the lack of suitable materials on the Rand for making the arc in one piece. The squared arc requires strengthening at the corners, and this is done with pieces of iron hooping, nails, or screws. The usual home-made *Timbila* has no nails or metal of any sort, but Katini, for example, has now taken to the squared arc even at home because he fancies he overcomes to a certain extent a tendency of the arc to twist when the support strings are tightened (Fig. I). The two ends of the arc are carved with patterns on top, *ucenyela* or *ukenyela*. Here again different makers favour their own special patterns. Single heads are also carved at the two ends of the arc, which are called *musungo* because it is on to them that the band for carrying the instrument is strung. This band is called *likole kupakata* and is sometimes made of hide or leather, but more usually of bark rope plaited into four strands, *nkuti yakuhora*.

The arc is completed ready to affix to the instrument by boring two holes, *matsoko*, in each end to fit over the tenons of the backbone, thus holding both itself and the legs firmly in place when the tension strings, *tiŋgoti*, are strained up.

Between the two ends of the instrument the notes, *timbila*, are suspended on these strings each over its own hole in the backbone. But the weight of the notes would be too great for the *tiŋgoti* unsupported, so they are kept in place and trim by small supports, *nyamaŋganani* (pl. *banyamaŋganani*), between every two notes (Fig. V). These light strips of wood are well carved with two heads, *musuŋgo*, at either end and are decorated on top. The decorations (*ucenyela*) are generally simple incisions made with a knife. The supports are fixed on to the backbone in the same way as the *matamba*, by burning small holes in both the backbone and the supports at the appropriate places and tying them with strings of bark fibre, *ŋgoti*. Two holes are also burned in them at the proper places through which the supporting strings of the notes are passed.

The whole frame of the instrument is now complete, ready for the notes themselves. One other operation can be completed while awaiting the notes and that is to prepare the vibrators on the resonators. This is a delicate job and, they say, is usually left to the last. Each resonator is bored with a small hole on the side nearer the player. The holes increase in size with the size of the resonator. In Katini's own *Saŋge* his vibrator holes vary from $\frac{5}{8}$ inch in the bass to $\frac{5}{16}$ inch in the treble. The final construction of the vibrators is left until the notes are tuned and the resonators are tuned in sympathy with each note.

The makers of *Timbila* all agree that this is the easier part of the instrument to make. Now they are faced with the more arduous job of making and tuning the notes, which is indeed a skilled job, though the construction of a good frame is by no means unskilled work.

The *mwenje* tree (*Ptaeroxylon obliquum*, Radlk., syn. *O. utile*, Sneezewood; identified by the Department of Forestry at Pretoria) is only found in one small region of the Zavala district in the areas of the minor chiefs, the Cabos Mahamba and Mangachilo, under Chief Zandamela, who is Regulo of this area. The trees grow in a thickly wooded portion of the country and are not very numerous. Chief Mahamba insisted that he had only four trees left, but I do not believe that this is strictly true. His neighbour, into whose country this belt of trees extends, has certainly a fairly large number of them. *Mwenje* is a very slow-growing wood, one of the hardest and heaviest known in southern Africa, and is heavily charged with oily resin. Most of the trees are small, little more than poles, and it is from these that the Chopi *Timbila* maker chooses his wood. The maker has to walk to the wood to select his timber, and in the case of the makers in the eastern part of the country this may mean a journey of forty miles or more each way. There is, they say, another area where the *mwenje* may be found in the Inharrime district to the east in the area under Chief Gwambini. But naturally the Chopi do not feel entitled to cut timber in this area outside their borders. This reluctance has given Regulo Zandamela a monopoly in *mwenje* which of recent years he has not hesitated to exploit. He demands from 10s. to £1 (50 to 100 escudos) for the right to make one cutting of timber. This tax has seriously threatened the manufacture of *Timbila* and the Administrador of the district was about to make investigations when he heard about it in 1943. Chief Zandamela excuses himself on the score that his old father, who was Zandamela before him, had on his death-bed given an injunction to his people to preserve the *mwenje* trees as they were getting scarcer. The old Chief had at the time one of the best orchestras in the country, which was mentioned by H. P. Junod many years ago. It was for the sake of the music that he expressed his concern for the trees and not, as his son has interpreted, for the benefit of his pocket. This son of old Mahlatini, as Zandamela was once called, is the one mentioned in the *Mzeno* of Gomukomu's 1940 *Ŋgodo*. He had been put in prison for insubordination and drunkenness.

The importance of a ready supply of this timber for making *Timbila* will be appreciated, as it is the most essential component of the instrument, and other woods have not the same resonant qualities. The inferior instruments found on the mines are made from scraps of all kinds of wood which are most unsuitable for the purpose. The mine musicians well know the limitations of their instruments, and spoke to me about it, wishing they had their home-made *Timbila* to play on instead of the crude substitutes which crack more easily and fail to produce the deep ringing notes which characterize a good xylophone.

To return to the process itself, the instrument maker, having completed his frame, now goes off on a two- or three-day expedition to the woods where he can cut *mwenje*. Having paid his respects and tax to the Regulo he is now entitled to cut the number of small trees he needs for making this one instrument or so. It appears from what they say that they prefer small trees to larger ones, though in either case the wood is so hard that it quickly blunts their axes. Those fortunate enough to get hold of one prefer to use a saw. Once felled, the log is sawn or cut into appropriate lengths for the instrument they are making and split down its centre, which often has a beautiful silky, light brown and yellow grain. One slat, *dikokoma*, is obtained from each half of the split wood, though for slats which form the higher notes and which are much smaller in width they say they can sometimes split a log into three or even four *makokoma*. The maker now chooses his slats, carefully arranging them according to size, and roughly trims them with his adze. Having obtained sufficient *makokoma* for his purpose, with a few over in case of breakages, by splitting and other accidents, he begins the curing process.

Curing is done by fire. A small trench is dug in the ground about 4 feet long, 10 to 12 inches wide, and about 12 inches deep. In this trench he makes a wood fire and when the flames have died down leaving only the red-hot embers he places the slats across the trench to heat. This heating first drives out all the sap and moisture and later, it appears, drives the oily resin into all the cells of the wood. As the timber is highly inflammable this process requires constant watching or the slats will catch alight and burn rapidly. The scorched marks you so often see on the notes of the *Timbila* are due to over-heating in this manner. The curing may take from one to two full days to complete according to the dampness of the wood. Every half-hour or so the fire has to be made up in order to keep it alive. The work is hot and exacting as the slats cannot be left for a moment in case they catch alight. While some of the slats are curing the maker continues to shape the others until by the time all are cured they are also fully shaped and graded in size from the smallest treble note to the broadest bass. I watched Katini at work curing his slats and it was quite remarkable how the process gradually improved the quality of the tone, which became richer and fuller as the resin presumably penetrated into all the cells, making the wood altogether homogeneous. *Mwenje* wood can be very trying to the worker as it is apt to have small cracks and fissures which, once they develop in the wood, completely ruin the tone and give rise to buzzing sounds and extraneous notes. Such slats have to be discarded.

Here it is necessary to describe the shape of a *Timbila* note, though anyone already acquainted with the notes of xylophones will be familiar with the general principles of making a slat of wood reverberate to a musical pitch. The *Timbila* notes of the Chopi are broader and somewhat longer than those of European xylophones. They are designed to be played by soft, not hard, beaters, and so the broad shape is necessary to bring out the true tone of the fundamental notes. The slat is cut with square ends in the shape of a shallow arch. The arch, *dipala*, is hollowed out with the adze on the under side (*msana*) (Fig. VI *a*) until the note falls to the required pitch. Should the maker take too much wood away it is possible to retrieve the situation by paring away the wood near the two ends, *itsoka*. This raises the pitch (Fig. VI *b*). The top *masuni* of the slat, which is now called *dikokoma*, is left smooth and flat, the edges are rounded, and they are finished by boning to a high polish. There remains now only the boring of the hole in the *dikokoma* by which it is made fast to the supporting strings in the instrument. This hole is usually cut square and not round, and is placed at the natural node where the musical vibrations in the wood are at their minimum. There are two such nodes approximately a quarter of the length of the slat from either end. The points of maximum vibration are in the centre and at each end. The support strings are so placed as to hold the slats at these 'dead' spots and so avoid muting the free vibration of the wood.

The slats are now ready for assembling into the instrument, and for final tuning. Until they are fixed in place they are still called *makokoma*, but as soon as they form part of the instrument they are *timbila*, notes, from which the whole instrument derives its name. With regard to the assembly of the notes, most instruments are assembled with bass on the left and treble on the right, as with us. But the *Timbila* is an accommodating instrument in that it can be adapted for left- or right-handed players. By reversing the arc to the opposite side and re-arranging the vibrators accordingly, the naturally left-handed player, *libaba*, can have his treble in the left hand and bass in the right. I have found about half a dozen left-handed instruments both in the Zavala district and on the Reef.

One of the early Portuguese writers on this part of Africa, the famous Friar João dos Santos, mentions this fact when writing about other Karanga natives who were living some three hundred miles farther north between the Sabi and the Puŋgwe rivers under Chief Quiteve. Their history must have been similar to that of the Chopi of the time, the fifteenth and sixteenth centuries. Both came under the influence of the Monomotapa, being members of the kingdom of Mocaranga. The kingdom appears to have been well established prior to the arrival of Chief Monomotapa himself a few years before the first Portuguese explorers. This 'Benjamite' branch of the family appears from dos Santos's account of 1586 to have assembled all its instruments left-handed.[1]

'The best and most musical of their instruments is called the *Ambira* which greatly resembles our organs; it is composed of long gourds, some very wide and some very narrow, held close together and arranged in order. The narrowest, which form the treble, are placed on the left, contrary to that of our organs, and after the treble come the other gourds with their different sounds of contralto, tenor, and bass, being eighteen gourds in all.'

The maker having cut, cured, and shaped his *makokoma* now carries them home for the final processes, including the skilled job of tuning.

It is interesting to note how the tuning is done. The result we have already discussed, but not the order in which the maker tunes his notes. He first makes his tone centre or tonic, *Hombe*. This central or key note is naturally the most important because all the rest are tuned from this pitch. Some of the makers claim that they can tell the exact pitch of the *Hombe* without reference to another instrument. I have tested them with my tuning-forks and the claim seems to be justified in many instances. I found just the same sureness of pitch in Shona musicians of Southern Rhodesia, and although insufficient data have as yet been collected to prove the point, there is reason to believe that they are as capable of defining their own familiar pitches as those of us who claim to have absolute pitch.

[1] G. M. Theal, *Records of South-Eastern Africa*, Government of the Cape Colony, vol. vii, p. 202.

Having tuned *Hombe*, the maker now tunes his scale up to the octave, every note in turn up the scale. He attempts to give each interval exactly the same value, and this accounts for the Chopi disregard for the true fourth and fifth which in other parts of Africa are often the first intervals to be tuned. Once the initial scale is complete up to the octave of *Hombe*, called by some *Hombe idoko*, the little Hombe, the musician runs over his notes and makes certain they are as even as he can get them. Then, from there onwards, the tuning of the remaining notes is done in octaves from this central scale. As a rule their octaves are true and exact.

The well-tuned notes are now assembled in pairs between the supports and tied down with two thongs which simply and effectively keep them in place and prevent them from touching each other when played. By passing the far thong through the hole in the note and so under the supporting string the note is prevented from slipping out. The near thong is wound over the notes and under the support string. When the player wishes to inspect the resonators below each note he undoes this near thong, which allows the note to be swung up without falling out of the instrument.

Now the tuning of the resonators remains to be done.

First the maker prepares his vibrators, *dikosi* (pl. *makosi*) (Fig. VII). The vibrators are small membranes fixed to a wax nipple on the side of the resonating chambers over the small holes which vary in size according to the size of the *matamba*. This is done by warming a short roll of wax by working it between the hands, and pressing it into place around a small, tapered wooden instrument, *ŋgwarotu* or *peniheni*, which is inserted into this hole. By careful shaping with the fingers a finely made nipple is formed about a quarter to half an inch high. The *peniheni* is withdrawn and the nipple covered with a small circular piece of membrane, *ivondo*. The membrane adheres firmly to the wax and is carefully pressed into place so that the whole vibrator is airtight. This membrane is made either from the diaphragm of the *kwewa*, a small jerboa, *ivondo ya kwewa*, or from the peritoneum of the ox. I have not seen them make the former, but the latter is carefully drawn from the intestines of the ox and placed on the maker's legs or arms to dry and stretch. When it is dry enough it is peeled off and carefully rolled up and put in a safe place. No Chopi

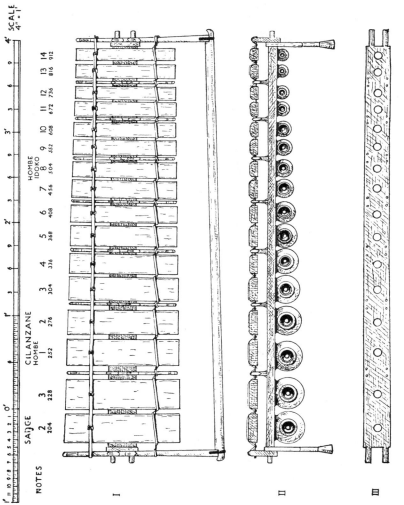

DIAGRAM VI. TIMBILA. SADGE, MADE BY KATINI NYAMOMBE, ZAVALA. P.E.A., about 1938

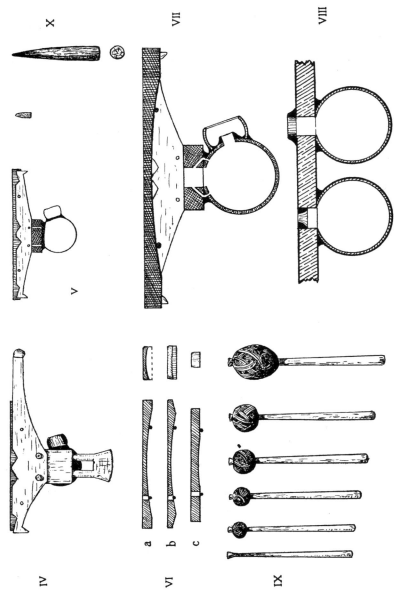

DIAGRAM VII. DETAILS OF KATINI'S SADGE. TIMBILA

musician is without his spare pieces of *ivondo* with which to repair his *makosi*. Farther north, bat's wing is commonly used, or even cigarette paper, and the egg sac of certain kinds of spider.

The *makosi* must not be too tight or they will not vibrate properly. A little pressure on the surface of the membrane with the thumb makes this right. The function of this vibrator is to nasalize the note, to give it an edge, and it is particularly effective for musical instruments which have to be played in the open air. But this is not all. The vibrator of itself gives the note reverberated in the gourd a certain quality, but it has to be rounded or the final result is too hard and blatant. This rounding of the note is achieved by placing a 'trumpet' around the *makosi*. It is called *mujuwawa* (pl. *siwawa*) and is also made of *ditamba* like the gourds. Its very name gives its function *wa wa*, the rounding of the buzzing sound from the unprotected vibrator. The *mujuwawa* also performs the necessary function of protecting the delicate membrane from damage, but its more important function is in producing a good round tone in the instrument. The *siwawa* are made from the shells of the fruit of the rubber tree, which are light and strong, or from the handles of cultivated gourds. They are fixed on to the surface of the resonating gourd by means of wax only, and are not sewn on, as one might expect. The reason for this is that they are more easily removed should the *makosi* need quick repairs, for without removing them one's fingers would not be able to get at the vibrator. The rounded fruit is cut off top and bottom, leaving a central circular segment which is ideal for producing a rounded note. The tins which are used on the Reef in place of these trumpets are straight-sided and therefore cannot give quite the same quality to the notes as the more mellow home-made *Timbila* have. The tonal quality of the instrument is partly dependent upon these little vibrator trumpets, a point which appears to have been overlooked, except by old Father André Fernandes.

I suggested to the makers that their vibrators might sound louder if they were placed on the other side of the resonators, the side away from the player. They said it would not make any difference to the sound, as the dancers would hear it just as well their way and the advantage of quick inspection by the player outweighed any other consideration, particularly as a note with a broken *dikosi* sounded dead and had to be mended at once.

Lastly, there remains the tuning of the resonators (Fig. VIII). This is done by one of two methods. The resonator as affixed to the instrument is either exactly in tune with its slat above or slightly sharp. If this is not so they take it off and cut it down until its cubic capacity is about right. Then any alteration to be made is done by adjusting the orifice of the resonator hole in the backbone. Some makers prefer to build up a neck of wax to increase the total capacity of the *ditamba* resonator, which has the effect of lowering its note; others achieve the same end by contracting the size of the hole with wax. This is also a well-known principle in tuning and is used by our own instrument makers, who employ a similar method in tuning certain kinds of organ pipes and resonating boxes.[1]

As the resonator is brought into tune with its *mbila* above it, the musical note swells out into a full round tone, very much louder than the note produced by the wood unaided. When tuning a note the maker often mutes the buzzer until he is certain that he has obtained the exact sympathetic resonance in the gourd. The note is sounded during tuning by continual blows from one or other of the rubber-headed beaters.

The tuning of the gourds is, of course, affected by temperature in the same way as all wind instruments are affected. The Chopi musicians well know the effect of heat upon the tone of their *Timbila*. That is why they dislike playing in the direct sun or at midday. Their instruments, they say, sound best in the early morning or late evening. This is true because the resonators are tuned in the shade at a moderate temperature. At higher temperatures the air in the resonator expands and so ceases to be in tune with its *mbila* which, being wood, is not affected to the same extent by a rise of temperature. The tone of the instrument is dependent upon the perfect sympathetic vibration of both the wooden slat and the air in the resonator. Without the sympathetic vibration of the column of air in the gourd, the vibrator would

---

[1] The principle of controlling the tuning of resonators is complicated, but it has been scientifically assessed. It depends upon a number of factors, including:
  (1) the density of the medium (air) which varies with the temperature;
  (2) the velocity of sound in the medium;
  (3) the area of the opening in the resonator;
  (4) the wave-length of the note to be recorded.
A change in any one of these factors alters the characteristic quality of the resonator and consequently the note which it will resound.

not sound, nor would the trumpet perform its function, and the result would be a sadly muted orchestra.

No wonder the Chopi still line up their orchestras in the shade of large trees, and still build their villages in the woods, 'in the darkest and most covered places', which Father André Fernandes deplored as unhealthy. They had a reason.

The Chopi are well aware of the natural laws controlling the production of sound in so far as their type of instrument is concerned. So they know full well that all beaters have not the same qualities, and carefully graded heads are needed to bring out the tone of a *Timbila*, from the very soft, large heads required for the double bass, *Gulu*, to the hard small heads used for the highest notes of the *Saŋge* and *Cilanzane*. The principle behind this fact is that a blow upon the surface of the *mbila* must immediately evoke the fundamental note by setting the wood in vibration. If a beater is too hard the shorter wave-lengths are evoked and the fundamental note may remain dead. This gives a crisp, thin sound associated with European xylophones. On the other hand, if the beater is too soft it will not evoke a note at all in the higher registers. For this reason you will find all Chopi players hold a slightly harder-headed beater in their right hands than in their left (except, of course, in the case of left-handed players). This means, over the whole orchestra, a gradation of beaters into six or seven degrees of hardness or softness—the softer the beater the larger its head (Fig. IX).

I have not witnessed the manufacture of beaters, *koŋgo* (pl. *tikoŋgo*), but this is how it was described to me. They first make the handle of the beater, *ndoŋga*, which may be made of any suitable wood, especially *mukusu*. This is carefully shaped, smoothed for comfortable handling, and nicely balanced, gradually tapering towards the head. At the head they slightly increase the diameter of the stick towards the tip so that the rubber head will not be inclined to fly off the handle. This is a difficulty experienced with the beaters made on the Rand from pieces of solid rubber cut from old conveyer-belts' rubber blocks or gaskets.

They next go into the woods to find the rubber vine, *mbuŋgo* or *ibuŋgo* (*Landolphia kirkii*), and they carefully make long incisions in the bark of the vine, which fill with sap. They prefer to do this in the afternoon and return the following morning, by which time the rubber has coagulated. They then find they can pull the rubber off in long strands. This is wound on to the handle of the beater with the correct tension to achieve the right degree of hardness or softness in the head, *ndandi*. The hard-headed beaters are wound tightly and the head left small, about an inch in diameter. The remainder are graduated in size and tension until the left-hand beater for *Debiinda* is about 2 inches in diameter. The beaters for *Zigulu* are much larger and may be from 3 to 4 inches across and very soft.

When a beater is newly wound the head appears to be made from sinews. It is easy to see how the early writers, such as dos Santos, mistook newly wound rubber for sinews, as it is unlikely that Europeans had any knowledge of the uses of rubber at that time and consequently would not have recognized it.[1]

The musicians have to be careful not to leave their beaters out in the sun as the raw rubber quickly perishes and becomes tacky. The large beaters for the double bass are particularly liable to perish as they are so lightly wound on to the sticks that they are often mere lumps of soft rubber. Some makers, in order to save rubber, start their heads by making a core of bark fibre. This is considered rather lazy by others, particularly as the core is apt to show through later on and spoil the quality of the beater.

From this it will be seen that a complete set of beaters suitable to bring out the full resonance of the four octaves of the combined *Timbila* comprises from five to six degrees of hardness in the heads: No. 1 a similar pair for *Gulu*, No. 2 (left hand) and No. 3 (right hand) for *Debiinda*; No. 3 (left hand) and No. 4 (right hand) for *Dole*, and similarly No. 4 and No. 5 for *Saŋge*; and No. 5 and No. 6 for *Cilanzane*.

From this description it will be seen that the work of manufacturing, tuning, and organizing the ensemble of *Timbila* is a considerable undertaking and demands enthusiasm, enterprise, and skill beyond the average in the African country-side. The work of a Chopi *Timbila* maker is never done. It is his constant joy and care.

[1] Fr. João dos Santos, 1856; G. M. Theal, *Records of South-Eastern Africa*, vol. vii, p. 202.

APPENDIX I

Extracts from Letters sent by the first Christian missionary to the Chopi, in 1560–2, Father André Fernandes

THIS very kindly sixteenth-century monk was the first missionary to the Chopi. André Fernandes stayed with them for just over two years until fever and poor food drove him out of the country and across to India where he died, many years later, much beloved and full of years. His brief observations on these people are most interesting to us, particularly his remarks about their music and national habits, which, as our translations of their modern poetry show, have changed very little in four hundred years. His short notes are necessarily incomplete—they are but excerpts from private letters—but when we remember his century it is remarkable how the truth of many of his sentences still shines across the years. When I think of the present-day Administrador, Dr. Luiz de Vasconcelos, shaking his head over the shortcomings of the Chopi chiefs under his charge, especially in this little matter of drink, my mind runs to the old monk of 1560 doing exactly the same in his day and writing to his friend that 'the chief was a very good man for a kaffir, but drank more than he could wish'; but loyally adding that this native chief whom he could not help liking was not so bad in comparison with some others he had heard of.

Although, from what he tells us, only five Portuguese; trading for the king and their captain, were settled at Inhambane, the small port near Cape Corrientes some 70 to 80 miles away, the native musicians seem to have made a fairly close study of their culinary habits. Father André Fernandes's first example of a native song in 1560 is strangely reflected in Katini's *Ŋgeniso* for his 1940 *Ŋgodo*, both of which have the food of the Portuguese as their theme.

There are several other interesting points in these letters from Gamba's country, many of which have quite unconsciously been confirmed by this study. Reference to the king's big drum, for example, is one. I have never before seen such large drums as are found amongst the Chopi. I managed to buy an old one from Nyakutowo's kraal for a collection of Bantu Musical Instruments. It measured 3 feet 9 inches tall and 26 inches across the head. It was lying in a disused hut and they had to pull the door-posts down to get it out for me.

Other points of interest in the Fernandes letters speak for themselves when read in conjunction with present-day songs.

Extracts from the book called 'Lendas da India'. (G. M. THEAL, *Records of South-Eastern Africa,* Vol. II)

24th June 1560. Letter from FATHER ANDRÉ FERNANDES *to the* FATHER PROVINCIAL OF INDIA

p. 62. Here [at Otongue] is a certain João Raposo, a mulatto born at Sofala, who has been in Portugal, and is now with me as interpreter.

p. 63. All the country belongs to this King Otongue, where they say there are ten or twelve thousand souls, in which there are heads of kraals, as in one his brother, and son-in-law, and nephew, and another the greatest of all, who came to take possession of his authority by the death of his father, is very well disposed and awaits our coming to receive baptism.

p. 64. All in this kingdom who are Mocarangas. . . .

p. 64. This kraal Otongue is situated on a great river which comes hither from the sea, and though there is no tide very near, there is a slight tide in the river. In the winter they say the water can be used for drinking, but not at present, because it is somewhat brackish.

p. 64. Millet is the best and chief part of their provisions and they use what would feed them for thirty days to make a drink called empombe for one occasion.

p. 65. They are peacefully inclined except when they are drunk. . . .

p. 65. These things [pictures] which appeal to their eyes make a great impression upon them . . . for which reason I have sent for a picture of the Judgment, which seems to me most suitable for them. . . .

They are more domesticated and friendly than you would think; . . . I greatly desire to introduce justice among them, and have some sort of a prison, and afterwards introduce such slight penalties as we can, and for this reason I greatly long to have the aforesaid picture of the Judgment here, with which to commence the work.

p. 66. This land seems to me the least fertile in the province, but it is peopled by the best inhabitants, for all the subjects of this king are Mocarangas, as I have said, and among the Kaffirs they are considered a better people than the Bongas, the greater part of Kaffraria being peopled by these two nations.

The Bongas are all circumcised, but not the former. The reason that these Mocarangas are among the Botongas, and surrounded by them on every side, is that the father of the present ruler had his domain in Bocolonga, and was at war with another more powerful than himself and was defeated.

His son, finding himself in this place with the men who remained after the defeat, fought with the ruler, and took possession of the land, and thus they remained among the Botongas.

APPENDIX I 145

He is a very good man for a Kaffir, but drinks more than I could wish; but the interpreter tells me he drinks very little in comparison to other chiefs he has seen among the Kaffirs.

p. 67. The country here is healthy, and would be more so if the Kaffirs would place their kraals along the seashore, where they would be refreshed by the sea-breezes. But they always choose the darkest and most covered places which they can find, under the largest trees, upon which they hang their provisions, so that no kraal of the Kaffirs can be healthy.

Letter from FATHER ANDRÉ FERNANDES *to* BROTHER LUIZ FROES *at the College of Goa. From Otongue, 25th of June 1560*

p. 76. The gallants of this country wear two horns on their heads, of which the foundation is made by dividing the hair, bringing half to the front and half at the back, and then they stick in two pieces of wood. . . .

. . . resembling painted devils, and of your charity, beloved brother, let the picture of the Judgement which I have asked for contain devils with horns.

Letter from FATHER DOM GONÇALO SILVEIRA *to the* FATHERS AND BROTHERS OF THE COLLEGE AT GOA. *Mozambique, 9th August 1560*

p. 95. Tongue is the chief town of Gamba whom we came to convert, and he is called king of Tongue.

Letter from FATHER ANDRÉ FERNANDES *to the* BROTHERS AND FATHERS OF THE SOCIETY OF JESUS IN PORTUGAL. *From Goa, 5th December 1562*

p. 142. These people [people of Tongue] are much given to the pleasures of singing and playing. Their instruments are many gourds bound together with cords, and a piece of wood bent like a bow, some large and some small, and to the openings in which they fasten trumpets with the wax of wild-honey to improve the sound, and they have their treble and bass instruments, &c.

At night they serenade the king and anyone who has made them a present, and he who makes the most noise is accounted the best musician.

Their songs are generally in praise of him to whom they are singing, as 'this is a good man, he gave me this or that, and will give me more'.

Two songs are in common use among them, one is 'Abenezaganbuia' which means that the Portuguese eat many things at the same time, or many different dishes, for they never eat of more than one thing at a time, and they never eat and drink at the same time, not from temperance, but from habit.

Sometimes they have drinking feasts which last three or four days, during which they eat nothing. Their wine is made from the fruit of the thickets; and of all their provisions they make some kind of drink, of which they are very fond, and one of them will drink more than three Germans.

The other song is: 'Gombe zuco virato ambuze capana virato', which means, the cow has leather for shoes and the goat has no leather for shoes; not because they wear shoes, for they all go barefoot unless the soles of their feet are sore, and they have to walk among prickly undergrowth, then they make soles of cow-hide and fasten them beneath their feet with straps.

Their dance represents all the actions of warfare, as surrounding the enemy, being surrounded, open warfare, conquering, being conquered, taking wood and water by force, and everything else which can occur in war, all very appropriately expressed.

Their dress for this feast is finer than for any other, for on this occasion they have skins of animals rather narrow with the tails attached, and these they tie round them so that when they twirl round on one foot, which they do with great lightness, the tails fly out in a large circle, and when one or two advance out of the ranks, they fly out with marvellous lightness and throw the sand into the air with their feet to such a height that it is hardly credible by those who have not seen it. This they also do directly a great man dies.

p. 143. Every death and illness is laid to the charge of something else, and to discover what the illness may be they cast lots with small shells ... and certain officials are appointed for this purpose.

p. 144. Generally when anyone dies, they consult certain wizards of the country who enjoy great credit, to learn who killed their parents or relations.

p. 144. Another whose wife left him was said to have died from that cause, and he who afterwards married her was sentenced to pay for it, which he did with a boy ... these demands are called milandos among them.

p. 149. There is another more solemn form of oath, which is only used at the command of the king, and this is to swear by the king's great war drum, which when they play upon it is heard at a distance of three or four leagues.

p. 150. Among these fortunate people I dwelt for two years and some months.

ANDRÉ FERNANDES

PLATE XV

'The old man is very fond of music'

The old man in question is fifth in the line, almost hidden by number four. Musicians of Chief Davida, an isolated small group of Chopi, living in the Manhiça district near Lourenço Marques, playing at the Administrador's office

APPENDIX II

Glossary of Words and Musical Terms connected with Timbila Orchestras

I. CHOPI–ENGLISH. CLASSIFIED

The Instrument

Timbila, pl. Timbila	instrument as a whole, xylophone, marimba
Cilanzane, Malanzane	treble xylophone or Timbila
Saŋge, Sanje	alto Timbila
Dole, Mbiŋgwe	tenor Timbila
Debiinda, Noni	bass Timbila
Gulu, Kulu, pl. Zikulu	double bass Timbila
Makokoma	practice Timbila made and played mostly by children. Made of muhesu wood. Slats rest on two rolls of grass or palm leaf. Played with wooden beaters

Parts of the Instrument

dikokoma, pl. makokoma	wooden slat of mwenje wood, before being fixed into the instrument
mbila, pl. timbila	note fixed in position in the instrument
masuni	top of the mbila or dikokoma
msana	back or lower side of mbila
dipala, kupala	arch, tuning-arch for lowering the pitch of the note
itsoka	outside ends of the mbila which are pared off underneath to raise the pitch of the note
detsoko, pl. matsoko	hole cut in the mbila through which a thong is threaded to keep it in place; hole in backbone for resonating gourds, in supports, &c.
mugwama	backbone of instrument
dinsoŋgola, itsoŋgola	tenons on either end of the backbone for attaching legs and arc
ditamba, pl. matamba	resonating gourd or chamber
ipula (ya pembe)	wax (of the ground bee), used in making the instrument

L

Parts of the Instrument—*continued*

kutoneto	to tune the resonating gourd by constricting orifice with wax or by building up a wax neck
kusuŋga kuŋgoti	to tie on with string, of the resonating gourd to the backbone, &c.
iŋgoti, pl. *tiŋgoti*	cord of hide or bark string, used for supporting the *timbila* slats in position; for straining up the instrument; for strapping down the, *timbila* &c.
murari (*kutsanisa timbila*)	arc and end straining bars combined (lit. for straining up the *timbila*)
nyamaŋganani, pl. *banyamaŋgani*	wooden support, distance piece placed between every two notes
ucenyela, ukenyela	carved decoration on the arc or supports
musuŋgo	carved head of arc or supports, lit. tie, place for tying on the cord for carrying instrument
dikosi, pl. *makosi*	vibrator, affixed to resonating gourd
ivondo (*ya kwewa*)	membrane, diaphragm of jerboa or peritoneum of ox, used for making the vibrator
kutumisa timbila, kuwambela timbila	to nasalize the note, to make a buzzing sound, to put an edge on the note by means of the vibrator, *dikosi*
mujuwawa, pl. *siwawa*	trumpet, protector for the vibrating membrane, *dikosi*
nenje, pl. *minenje*; *neŋge*, pl. *mineŋge*	leg of the instrument
mkondo	foot of the leg
likhole (*kupakata*)	band for carrying the instrument, attached to the *musuŋgo* of the arc, of bark rope or leather
nkuti yakuhora	bark rope plaited in four strands, to make the *likhole*

Tools

dibono	scraper
njivatelo	adze used in making *timbila*

mbato	home-made chisel for cutting out holes, *matsoko*
ntombo, ndombo	metal spike for burning out small holes
ŋgwaruto, peniheni	wooden tool, tapered to a point, for making holes, working the wax, making *makosi*
mbalahuta	rough leaves of a tree, used as sandpaper, for smoothing wood

Beaters, Rattle

koŋgo, pl. *tikoŋgo*	beater
undandi	head of beater, made of rubber, or cloth and bark string
mbuŋgo, ibuŋgo	rubber, from the rubber vine
ndoŋga	handle, stick of the beater
njele, njela	rattle made of gourd or tin with seeds inside

Musicians and Dancers

muveti, pl. *vaveti; muvete*, pl. *vavete*	player, musician
musiki watimbila; muveti watimbila	leader of the orchestra, composer, maker of *timbila*
musinye, pl. *basinye; musinyi*, pl. *basinyi*	dancer
muniŋgeti wabasinyi *mbandi wamabandla*	dance leader, composer of dance steps or routines
mdoto wanjele	rattle player
igodo, Iŋgodo, Mugodo, Iŋgodo	whole orchestra, players and dancers; orchestral dance, music for ballet

Musical Terms

msaho	musical competition, combined performance by several orchestras
dipṣui, pl. *mapṣui*	note, musical sound
kululama	to be in tune
kululamisa	to tune
kupambana	to be out of tune
kupambanisa	to put out of tune
Hombe	tonic, tone centre, note from which the others are tuned

MUSICAL TERMS—*continued*

hombe idoko	note an octave above *Hombe*
kanyamboswe	bass, bass notes, left hand
kanyadye	treble, treble notes, right hand
magumo kanyamboswe	lowest note in bass, end note of left hand
magumo kanyadye	highest note of treble, end note of right hand
madiyo	a wrong note
diŋgenile	true, in tune, a note in tune, true note
didoto, didoko	sharp, a note that is sharp
dahombe	flat, a note that is flat
mapṣui	melody, lit. notes, the notes of a tune
kuveta mapṣui	to play the melody
rondo	scale, the notes up the scale
sumeto	notes down the scale
kusumeto	to play the air, or tune, which is generally of a declining nature; falling notes, notes in a downward sequence
kudiŋgana	harmony, to play in harmony, to play an appropriate part in harmony with another
kudala	descant or high part
kuhambana	a part, contra-melody, a different part taken by another player
kuveta digando dimwedo	to play in unison
digando dimwedo	unison
indando, pl. *dindando*	tune, measure, phrase, sentence
kudiŋganisa	octave, to play in octaves
kuembelela	to sing, a verse (singing). See *diviŋgwa*
kuembelela vootsi	to sing together
kukata kuembelela	first verse (singing)
wombidi kuembelela	second verse (singing)
kuveta necibaba	to play with the left hand
kuveta necinɵne	to play with the right hand
kuhambaniswa mapṣui	to play with hands apart, one in treble and one in bass, hands well apart.

kumananisa	to play in the middle register, to cross over the hands while playing, to play the same note with each hand alternately
kunamisa	to play slower, rallentando
kunama	to play quietly, lit. looking down
kuvelusa	to indicate (by the leader) the end of a movement or the beginning of another; indication or sign; introductory bar or phrase
kuveta dikokoma dimwedu	to indicate (by the leader) by striking one note out loud
kuvetani vootsi or *mootsi*	to play together, to start to play together, entry of the full orchestra
kugwita nedigando dimwedo	to end a passage on octaves
kuniŋgeta (*indando*)	to start a tune by the leader, a solo, a cadenza, improvisation; a statement of the melody, theme to be played
kubala, kusaiya, kuſaiya	to count the number of measures between dance movements or verses
kuvetsamba	to play a note repeatedly, a repeated note
kutsambisela	to play trilling notes, trilling notes played very rapidly
ŋgutu	loud, forte or fortissimo
kuveta ŋgutu	to play loudly
kahombe	mezzoforte, fairly loud
kakudoko	soft, piano
kuleŋga	very softly, pianissimo
dikukwa	a clear note, without vibrator
cigubu, pl. *zigupu*	heavy pulse or beat
jikite, pl. *zikite*	light pulse, small beat
kukata indando *kudala* *kusumeta* or *kutsumeta* *kuniŋgeta*	four stages in introducing a movement by the leader: (1) play the air; (2) play high descant or cadenza; (3) to come down the instrument, descent; (4) to start the melody
kuvagela	to repeat a measure
cikuluveta	fast tempo
cikuluvetisa	very fast tempo

MUSICAL TERMS—*continued*

ndota	slow
kukata (indando)	to compose (a tune), to improvise
kuniŋgeta (kusinya)	to compose (steps for dancing)
weiŋgisa indando	to compose a dance routine
kuweŋgisa	to set dance steps to music
diviŋgwa, pl. *maviŋgwa*	verse, also solo dance measure
indando yawukoma	song for the chiefs, national song, national anthem, such as the Portuguese or British anthems

DANCE TERMS

msahone	place for dancing, or musical performances
kubandwa	imaginary centre line dividing dance-floor into two halves; when dancers divide they do so to left and right of this line
mabandwa	sections of dancers
katela hagari	to divide the dancers into sections
ciklavaŋgu, kavi	shield, dance shield
mgwawa	stick through shield
ditfari	dance spear-blade, dance stick
muceka kahalani	yellow cloth worn by dancers
pitula, mpepo	whistle used by dance leader
faduku, mkwasi	head bands worn by dancers
didowo	jackal-skin cape worn by dancers
ciwaka (pl. *si-*)	leggings of angora goat skin (lit. *sikumba wasiwaka capoŋgo*)
makara	solo shake
cigaza	solo dance action, rippling buttocks
kutsatsula	solo dance action, with either buttock
kusinya makara	to dance a solo shake, to gesture with hand and shoulders, upper body movement
kugavula, vugavula	solo dance, *pas seul*
vemile	standing still in preparation for a dance routine
kupetudza	to hold up the arms and shields above the head
ututa	to stand still during a dance, as in *Mzeno*, at attention

APPENDIX II

kuziŋginikela	to sway on alternate feet
kukavula	wild dance with high kicks and leaping
kucuia	quiet dance with pointing gestures
rirendu	dancing in line
masuni	dancing in file
kutsula masuni	to dance forward
kuuya misana	to dance backwards
kusuŋgameta	to mime with one hand while singing
kupeka hahatsi (*ha'atsi* or *haatsi*)	to bang the shield on the ground
kuzumbila hahatsi	to crouch down on the ground, to place shields on the ground
wonama	to bow down while dancing
ciklavaŋgu hahatsi nicitimwe	to swing the shields down and up
kundaka	to leap into the air
kupetula	to blow the whistle, indication to dancers
kutsatsula	a solo dance as done by the rattle players, with shaking buttocks, either right or left
kucaca njela	to play the rattle
mbamdidi basinyako	to dance in pairs
ukulhakuzela	solo dance by leader with cries

II. ENGLISH–CHOPI. ALPHABETICALLY

adze (for making xylophone)	*njivatelo*
air: to play the a., descending melody	*kusumeto*
arc, distance piece and straining bar complete, of xylophone	*murari*
armlet	*dicowa*
axe	*nzanga*
backbone of xylophone, main support	*mugwama*
band of leather or rope for carrying xylophone	*likhole*
bang, *v.t.*: to b. shield on the ground	*kupeka hahatsi*
bark: rope of b. used as band	*nkuti*
bass: bass notes, notes in left hand	*kanyamboswe*
beat, *n.*: heavy b.	*cigubu*, pl. *zigupu*
light b.	*jikite*, pl. *zikoŋgo*, pl. *tindandi*
beater	
head of b.	
handle of b.	*ndoŋga*

bow, *n.*: to bow down in dancing	*wonama*
buzz, *v.t.*	*kuwambela*
cadenza	*kuniŋgeta*
cape, *n.* of jackal skin	*didowo*
carving, carved decorations	*ukenyela*
chisel, *n.*	*mbato*
cloth: yellow c. worn by dancers	*muceka kahalani*
competition of players and dancers	*msaho*
compose, *v.t.* tune, improvise	*kukata*
c. steps for dancing	*kuniŋgeta*
c. dance routines with music	*weiŋgisa indando*
composer: of music	*musiki*
of dances	*muniŋgeti*
contra-melody	*kuhambana*
cord for supporting slats, straining up instrument, &c.	*iŋgoti*, pl. *ti-*
count, *v.t.*: bars, repeats, &c.	*kubala, kusaiya, kuʃaiya*
crouch, *v.i.*: to c. down on the ground while dancing	*kuzimbila hahatsi*
dance, *n.*: children's d.	*ŋgalaŋga*
n.: orchestral d.	*ŋgodo*, pl. *migodo*
n.: solo d.	*vugavula, cigaza, kutsatsula*
n. & v.i.: wild d. with high kicks and leaping	*kukavula*
n. & v.i.: quiet d. with pointing gestures	*kucuia*
v.i.: d. forward	*kutsula masuni*
v.i.: d. backwards	*kuuya misana*
dance-floor	*msahone*
dancer	*musinyi*, pl. *barirendu*
dancing, *n.*: d. in line	*masuni*
d. in file	
d. in pairs	*mbambidi basinyako*
decoration, carving	*ukenyela*
descant, high part, high treble	*kudala*
discord	*madiyo*
division of dancers into two sections	*katela hagari*
end, *v.t.*: to e. a passage on unisons or octaves	*kugwita nedigando dimwedo*
entry of full orchestra	*kuvetani vootsi* (or *mootsi*)

APPENDIX II

fast: f. tempo	*cikuluveta*
very f. tempo	*cikuluvetisa*
file: dancing in f.	*masuni*
flat (of pitch)	*dahombe*
foot of leg of xylophone	*mkondo*
forte, loud	*ŋgutu*
gauge for making vibrator nipples	*ŋgwaruto, peniheni*
gesture, *v.i.*: g. with hands and shoulders	*kusinya makara*
gourd: resonating g.	*ditamba*, pl. *ma-*
harmony, *n.*	*kudiŋgana*
to play in h., harmonize	*kudiŋgana*
head, of distance pieces of the xylophone, used as place to tie strap	*musuŋgo*
headband worn by dancers	*faduku, mkwasi, ciŋgundu*
hole in backbone, slats, &c.	*detsoko*, pl. *ma-*
improvisation	*kuniŋgeta*
indicate, *v.t.*	*kuvelusa*
indication: by leader	*kuvelusa*
by playing one note out loud	*kuveta dikokoma dimwedo*
to dancers	*kupetula*
jackal: j.-skin cape of dancers	*didowo*
key: key note	*hombe*
knife	*civatelo*
leader: of orchestra	*musiki watimbila*
of dancers	*muniŋgeti wabasinyi, mbandi wa mabandla*
leap, *n. & v.i.*	*kundaka*
left-handed	*libaba*
leg of xyiophone	*nenji*, pl. *mi-*; *neŋge*, pl. *mi-*
leggings of dancers	*ciwaka*, pl. *si-*
line: centre l. dividing dance-floor	*kubandwa*
dancing in l.	*rirendu*
loud: forte	*ŋgutu*
maker of instruments	*muwati*
measure, *n.*: musical sentence or song	*indando*, pl. *di-*

melody	*mapṣui*
contra-melody	*kuhambana*
to play m.	*kuweta mapṣui*
membrane, vibrator, made from the intestines of the jerboa, peritoneum of ox, &c.	*ivondo*
mezzoforte, fairly loud	*kahombe*
mime, *n. & v.i.*	*kusuŋgameta*
musician	*muveti*, pl. *va-muvete*, pl. *va-*
nasalize, *v.i.* buzz	*kuwambela timbila*
national song, anthem	*indando yawukoma*
note: bass n.	*kanyamboswe*
clear n. without vibrator	*dikukwa*
flat n.	*dahombe*
highest n. in treble	*magumo kanyadye*
lowest n. in bass	*magumo kanyamboswe*
musical sound	*dipṣui*, pl. *ma-*
repeated n.	*kuwetsamba*
sharp n.	*didoto, didoko*
slat in position in xylophone	*mbila*, pl. *ti-*
treble n.	*kanyadye*
true n., in tune	*diŋgenile*
wrong n.	*madiyo*
notes: ascending	*rondo*
descending	*sumeto*
trilling or tremolo	*kutsambisela*
octave, *n. & v.i.*: to play in octaves	*kudiŋganisa*
note an o. above key note or tone centre, *Hombe*	*hombe idoko*
orchestra, players and dancers	*iŋgodo, ŋgodo, mugudo, igodo*
orchestral dance	*ŋgodo*, pl. *migodo*
part, contra-melody	*kuhambana*
pas seul, solo dance	*kugavula, vugavula*
phrase, musical p.	*indando*, pl. *di-*
play, *v.t.* (music)	*kuweta*
air or melody	*kuweta mapṣui*
in octaves	*kudiŋganisa*
in unisons	*kuweta digando dimwedo*
loudly	*kuweta ŋgutu*
softly	*kunama*

APPENDIX II

play, with left hand, in bass	*kuweta necibaba*
with right hand, in treble	*kuweta necinene*
with hands well apart, one in treble and one in bass	*kuhambaniswa mapṣui*
in middle register	*kumananisa*
with hands crossed	*kumananisa*
same note with alternate hands	*kumananisa*
a note repeatedly	*kuwetsamba*
rallentando, slower	*kunamisa*
together, of full orchestra	*kuwetani vootsi*
v.t.: play rattle	*kucacha njele*
player: of xylophone (*timbila*)	*muweti*, pl. *va-*; *muwete*, pl. *va-* (*watimbila*)
of rattle	*mdoto*
pulse, *n.*: heavy p. or beat	*cigubu*, pl. *zigupu*
light p. or beat	*iikite*, pl. *zikite*
raise, *v.t.*: r. hands and shields above the head	*kupetudza*
rallentando	*kunamisa*
rattle, *n.*	*njele, njela*
v.t.	*kucacha njele*
r. player	*mdoto wanjele*
repeat, *n. & v.t.*: a measure or phrase	*kuwagela*
repeated note	*kuwetsamba*
rope, bark rope	*nkuti yakuhora*
rubber, raw rubber	*mbuŋgo*
scale: ascending notes, up the s.	*rondo*
descending notes, down the s.	*sumeto*
sections of dancers	*mabandwa*
sentence: musical s.	*indando*, pl. *di-*
set, *v.t.*: s. dance steps to music	*kuweŋgisa*
shake, *n.*: solo s.	*makara*
v.t.: to dance a shake	*kusinya makara*
sharp, *n. & adj.*: of (pitch)	*didoto, didoko*
shield, *n.*: dance s.	*kavi, ciklavaŋgu*, pl. *si-*
to bang s. on the ground	*kupeka hahatsi*
to place s. on the ground	*kuzumbila hahatsi*
to swing s.s up and down	*siklavanga hahatsi nicitimwe*
shield stick, through centre of s.	*mgwawa*
sign, *n. & v.i.*: indication for change in music, to signal or indicate intentions	*kuvelusa*

sing, *v.i. & v.t.*	*kuembelela*
s. together	*kuembelela vootsi*
slat, note before fixing into xylophone	*dikokoma*, pl. *mamasuni*
top of s.	*msana*
back or lower side of s.	*dipala, kupala*
arch of s. for lowering pitch	*itsoka*
ends of s. paired off to raise pitch	*detsoko*, pl. *mandota*
hole cut in s.	
slow, tempo	*kakudoko, kunama*
soft, softly, piano	*kuleŋga*
pianissimo, very s.	
solo: s. dance	*vugavula, kugavula*
played by leader	*kuniŋgeta*
s. shake	*makara*
s. dance by rattle player	*kutsatsula*
s. dance by dance leader	*ukulhakuzela*
song	*indando*, pl. *diditʃari*
spear: dance s.	
spike, *n.*: (for burning holes)	*ntombo*
stand, *v.i.*: s. still in preparation for dance routine	*vemile*
s. still during a dance such as *Mzeno*	*ututa*
start, *v.t.*: to s. a tune or measure by the leader	*kuniŋgeta*
stick: s. through shield	*mgwava*
dance s.	*ditʃari*
supports placed between each pair of notes on xylophone	*nyamaŋganani*, pl. *banyakuziŋginikela*
sway, *v.i.*: s. on alternate feet	
swing, *v.t.*: to s. shields up and down	*siklavaŋgu hahatsi*
tempo, fast	*cikuluveta*
very fast	*cikuluvetisa*
slow	*ndota*
tenons, on either end of backbone of xylophone	*dinsoŋgola, itsoŋgola*
tie, *n.*: place for tying on a strap	*musuŋgo*
tone centre, tonic	*hombe*
treble: t. note, right hand	*kanyadye*
tremolo, *n. & v.i.*	*kutsambisela*
trill, *n.*: trilling notes, vibrant playing	*kutsambisela*
trumpet, *n.*: protector for vibrators	*mujuwawa*, pl. *siwawa*

APPENDIX II

tune, *n.*	*indando*, pl. *didingenile*
in tune, true note	
v.i.: to be in t.	*kululama*
v.t.: to t. a slat or note	*kululamisa*
to t. a resonator	*kutoneto*
v.i.: to be out of t.	*kupambana*
v.t.: to put out of t.	*kupambanisa*
tutti, entry of full orchestra	*kuvetani vootsi*
unison	*digando dimwedo*
verse, *n.*: of singing	*kuembelela*
of playing, a measure or round	*diviŋgwa*, pl. *makukata kuembelela*
first verse	
second verse	*wombidi kuembelela*
vibrator, *n.*: of membrane	*dikosi*, pl. *ma-*
wax, *n.*: bees-w. for tuning, airtight joints, &c.	*ipula* (*yapembe*)
whistle, *n.*	*pitula, mpepo*
v.i.: as indication to dancers	*kupetula*
xylophone	*timbila*, s. & pl.
treble x.	*cilanzane, malanzane*
alto x.	*saŋge*
tenor x.	*dole, mbiŋgwe*
bass x.	*debiinda*
double-bass x.	*gulu, kulu*, pl. *zikulu*
children's practice x.	*makokoma*

APPENDIX III

List of Chopi Orchestras on the Witwatersrand
August 1944

(Kindly supplied by the Witwatersrand Native Labour Association, Ltd., Johannesburg)

Mine	No. of orchestras	No. of players
Brakpan	1	23
City Deep	1	17
C.M.R.	3	32
Crown Mines	2	20
Daggafontein	1	30
Durban Deep	3	50
East Champ d'Or	1	3 (Not active)
East Dagga	3	40
E. R. P. M.	—	4 (Not active)
Geduld	1	10
Geldenhuis Deep	1	14
Government Areas	1	40
Grootvlei	1	26
Langlaagte Estate	2	65
Luipaards Vlei	1	6
Marievale	—	6 (Not active)
Modder B.	2	26
Modder Deep	1	25
Modder East	1	7
New Kleinfontein	1	13
New Modder	1	12
Randfontein Estates	2	20
Rand Leases	2	25
Reitfontein Consolidated	—	4 (Not active)
Robinson Deep	1	14
Rose Deep	1	14
Simmer & Jack	1	20
S.A. Lands	1	26
Springs Mines	2	24
Sub Nigel	2	24
Van Dyk	1	31
Van Ryn Deep	2	24
Venterspost	1	20
Vogelstruisbult	1	12
West Rand Consolidated	1	20
Witwatersrand Deep	—	8 (Not active)
Witwatersrand G.M.	1	25
Total	**47**	**780**

Note. The orchestras marked 'Not active' are temporarily short of players or a leader, and are consequently unable to perform until more players return from the country. Four mines without orchestras are not listed.

APPENDIX IV

Analysis of a typical Chopi Orchestral Movement

8th Movement, MZENO of the ŊGODO, composed by GOMUKOMU of Filippe Banguza's Village, 1940

THE question of how to write down African music satisfactorily must remain an open one for many years to come. So this attempt to demonstrate in diagrammatic form the shape of a Chopi orchestral work must not be taken as a form of notation, but rather as a convenient method of conveying the information in symbols which can be reproduced on any typewriter.

In transcribing their music on to our staff, allowance must be made for the fact that our scale is not of course in tune with theirs and the transcription is made in terms of the nearest European equivalent (see Diagram V). It calls for the use of a tablature in its sixteenth-century sense, a statement indicating what tuning to adopt in order to play the piece of music as written.

In another sense, the diagram I have devised for our present purpose is also a tablature in itself.[1]

Later on I hope to be able to acquire a recording device which will mark on paper, after the style of a pianola recorder, the exact layout of an orchestral work in all its parts, self-recorded by the players as they perform. We shall then be able to ascertain, without fear of contradiction or inaccuracy, exactly what the Chopi musicians are playing. It is a tremendous task at present to attempt to analyse in detail, and quite frankly it is beyond most of us. The special recorder will simplify the problem for everyone and will also ensure a complete picture. The few bars we have now written of this one number which I have recorded represent many hours of careful listening and checking, most of it in the presence of the Chopi composer, Gomukomu.

The work is seen to be composed of regular parts which fit into each other in a well-ordered plan.

LEITMOTIVE or SUBJECT (Vocal). The basic melody of the lyric with certain variations dependent upon the speech tones of the words in each line. There are five melodic variations, contra-subjects. In this case and in most cases the first verse is sung to the leitmotive, followed by the other verses sung to one or other of the contra-subjects. The song only makes its appearance in the latter half of the movement, after the dance routine.

[1] See *The Oxford Companion to Music*, Percy A. Scholes, Second American Edition, Oxford, p. 916, 'Tablature'.

ORCHESTRAL GROUND. The basic ground played by the orchestra with a great number of set variations and free improvisations by individual players (when allowed). It is in two sections of four bars each, marked (*a*) and (*b*). This is repeated continuously from the *Tutti* to the coda, and like the wheels of a locomotive carries the whole performance smoothly and surely along. Against this background each of the solo parts is silhouetted. The dance routines are fitted into an exact number of repeats of the measure or ground. An orchestral variation, therefore, is encompassed by the eight bars of this measure, as with a chaconne or passacaglia.

ORCHESTRAL MOTIVE, or SENTENCE. Against the ground provided by the full orchestra we find the leader playing a full melodic sentence of sixteen bars, in two halves of eight bars, generally introduced by a phrase of four bars. (This is marked 'OM phrase' and 'OM Sentence'. When played by Gomukomu in octaves it is marked 'in ovs.'.)

INDICATIONS BY LEADER. These are given by the leader, as a rule fortissimo, during the latter half (*b*) of the orchestral ground. The orchestra then plays three repeats of the ground before making the change either to start the song or to play the coda. This is the *kuvelusa*, and is marked 'indication'.

TREBLE VARIATION. This variation or descant by the player of the *Cilanzane*, treble xylophone, is always a feature of the *Mzeno* movement. It usually, though not always, approximates to the vocal leitmotive or the melody of the words in the first line of the next verse, and is played during the pause between verses in the space of one or more orchestral grounds. (Marked 'Treb. Var.'.)

VOCAL INDICATION. During the singing of the lyric a single voice is heard to call out a word or two immediately after the end of each verse. It is the voice of the orchestral leader who sings the first word or two of the next verse to be sung by the dancers. In this way he usually calls for a repeat of each verse but is at liberty to name his next verse as he pleases and so cut out repeats. For purposes of recording this has to be done in order to keep within the time limit of a 10-in. or 12-in. record. When the last verse has been sung he will call out the first words of the opening verse, which tells the dancers of the approach of the coda, which is usually, though not always, a repeat of the whole or part of this verse.

LYRIC. The lines of the verses are numbered. Each verse, with the exception of the coda, is repeated twice. It will be noticed how, after the second singing of lines 5, 6, and 7, the Treble Variation is held for two instead of one measure of the ground (Nos. 53 and 54).

APPENDIX IV 163

DANCE ROUTINE. Unfortunately no notes were taken at the time of the dance routine which accompanied this movement, so the picture is incomplete in this particular. The dancers start with the full orchestra at the *Tutti*, and slowly advance towards the orchestra so that by the time the leader gives them the *kuvelusa* indication for the beginning of the song they are halted within two paces of the players, ready to sing in unison.

RATTLES. The rattle players play their rattles to enhance the rhythm from the *Tutti* onwards, but with all *Mzeno* movements they cease to play as soon as the singers are about to sing, and start again to play for the coda, which is performed fortissimo.

Lyric for the 8th MZENO Movement, GOMUKOMU, *1940*

1. Lavanani micaŋga sika timbila tamakono.
2. Howotawa ditsimbirini kavaluŋgu.
3. Ŋguyusa mwana atu kunevuneti timbila tamakono.
4. Nopwata Mzeno uuwa timbila.
5. A-koŋga ko nimafuiye Gomukomu watu,
6. A-koŋga ko nimafuiye Gomukomu watu,
7. Kwalakanya nyumbani kamina ko nopemberuke noka.
8. Maninya Mtumbu vasumako kutsura nikubilivila.
9. Maninya Mtumbu vasumako kutsura nikubilivila,
10. Mane woruwala cibembe ciya cawulombe.
11. Dabwa Lakeni wadanwa nkoma.
12. Filipe, mwana atu, unagwita unkudava ŋgwaluŋgu.
13. Awi Lakeni, wakuruma ako mahuŋgu akutala.
14. Awi Lakeni, wakuruma ako mahuŋgu akutala,
15. O upsala kudoŋgola nesiŋgaŋgo.
16. UaZandameleni madanwa mahuŋgu.
17. Ŋgoŋgondo utavile mahuŋgu ŋgundawa yakusela.
18. Lavanani micaŋga sika timbila tamakono.

Symbols used in the Tablature

Leader playing his *Timbila*	: - - - - - - - - - -
Treble Xylophone's Descant	: - - - : - - - :
Leader sings	: ooooooo
Singers, with number of line	(12) Filipe - - - -
	: oooooooooooo
Orchestra playing, each pulse, in 2/4 time	a b :...:...:...:...:...:

M

164   CHOPI MUSICIANS

Ground or measure numbered below orchestra line	: ... : ... : ... : ... : ... : 47
Rattles, each pulse every second beat	* * * * * * * *
Subjects and counter-subjects by singers	S 1, S 2, S 3, &c.

Published Records of Timbila *Music*

Since the first publication of this book and the foundation of the International Library of African Music, I have made many recordings of Chopi music, nineteen of which are now published by the I.L.A.M., P.O. Box 138, Roodepoort, Transvaal, South Africa, in the 'Sound of Africa' Series (12-in. long-playing records) under these numbers: TR. 1, 2, 5, 6, 11 and 197–210.

More specifically, recordings of some of the movements of the *migodo* described in this book can be found as follows:

P. 15	*Mzeno* 'Manganakana' from Katini's *mgodo* (1940)	TR–210.A.4	(rec. 1943)
	Mzeno 'Manganakana' from Katini's *mgodo* (1940)	TR–208.A.3	(rec. 1949)
P. 19	*Mgodo* of Katini (1943)	TR–209.A.1 to 8, B1	(rec. 1943)
	The *mzeno* 'Hinganyengisa' from this *mgodo*	TR–208.B.9	(rec. 1949)
	The *mzeno* 'Hinganyengisa' from this *mgodo*	TR–197.B.1	(rec. 1963)
P. 34	*Mzeno* 'Lavanani michanga' from Gomukomu's *mgodo* (1940)	TR–210.A.1, repeated on TR–204.B.1	(rec. 1943)
	Mzeno 'Lavanani michanga' from Gomukomu's *mgodo* (1940). L & R hand analysis	TR–210.A.2	(rec. 1943)
	Mzeno 'Lavanani michanga' from Gomukomu's *mgodo* (1940). In two different keys	TR–207.B.4 & 5	(rec. 1949)

Note: Appendix IV, V and VI, give an analysis, score and tablature of this item.

P. 39	*Mgodo* of Gomukomu (1942/3)	TR–209.B.2 to 8	(rec. 1943)
	The *mzeno* 'Hingane malala' from this *mgodo*	TR–210.A.3	(rec. 1943)

APPENDIX V

Musical Transcriptions

THE end of each repeat of the 'ground' on which these compositions are based is indicated by the double bars. The bars themselves have been taken to be two rattle beats long. This is only a convenience; this subdivision is not significant to the Chopi.

The special clef sign at the beginning of each line indicates that this music is written for the Chopi *timbila*. While for general purposes it may be taken as similar to the treble clef, *the notes are not the same*. Written 'middle C' here means *Hombe*, the lowest note of the *Cilanzane timbila*; written 'G above middle C' means *Canu*, the fifth note up from Hombe, etc. The exact pitches, in v.p.s., of various villages can be found on p. 125.

In the mzeno '*Lavanani* . . .' the left hand part and the song have been written out in compound time, 12/32. This is merely for rhythmic accuracy in relating the left and right hand parts to each other. In point of fact the left hand part sounds and feels exactly like simple 2/8 duple time. For easier reading imagine one dot removed from each note.

Where alternative notes occur, they are shown in square brackets.

ANDREW TRACEY

Lavanani Micangasika Timbila Tamakono by Gomukomu

Solo introduction to the Mzeno from his Mgodo of 1940, played on a 'sanje' mbila. See p. 34.

Transcribed by ANDREW TRACEY, from TR.210.A.1.

Lavanani Micangasika Timbila Tamakono by Gomukomu

Basic form of the accompaniment, as played by Gomukomu in the analytical recording TR.210.A.2. Variations marked in brackets, all for R.H.

Transcribed by ANDREW TRACEY.

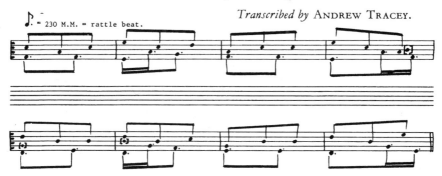

Lavanani Micangasika Timbila Tamakono by Gomukomu

Descant part played by Gomukomu on TR.210.A.1. Apart from 4 bars at the beginning and 3 at the end, L.H. and R.H. is not indicated. The right hand probably leads in most cases, however.

Transcribed by ANDREW TRACEY.

Lavanani Micangasika Timbila Tamakono by Gomukomu

The song, as it was sung on TR.210.A.1 without its normal repeats, showing, in small notes, how the leader lines the first words of the next verse. See p. 34.
An orchestral introduction precedes this transcription.

Hinganyengisa Masingita by Katini

Mzeno from his mgodo of 1943. Examples of the accompaniment on four different pitches of timbila.

Transcribed from live playing by ANDREW TRACEY. See p. 24.

4. DIBIINDA. From Sajoni, at Rand Leases Mine, Johannesburg, 1963.

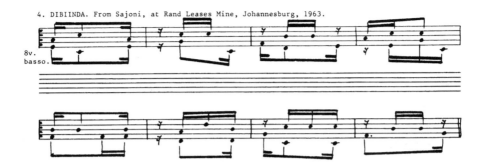

Hinganyengisa Masingita

The song, as sung on TR.209.A.7. See p. 24.
An orchestral introduction precedes this transcription.

Transcribed by ANDREW TRACEY.

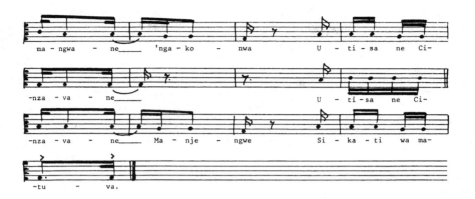

APPENDIX VI

TABLATURE OF THE MZENO MOVEMENT OF THE ŊGODO BY GOMUKOMU
at Banguza's village, Zavala, Portuguese East Africa, 1940

	Cadenza (f)	*kukata*		*kukala*
Leader	//: -------	------- :	------- :	------- :

	kusumeta	Introduction *kuniygeta*	*kuwelusa*	(ff)
Leader	: -------	------- :	------- :	---v-v-:
Orchestra				a *Tutti* b
				1
Rattles				* * * * * * * * * *

(f) a OM sentence

	OM phrase			
Leader	: -------	------- :	------- :	------- :
	a	b	a	b
Orchestra	: · · · ·	· · · · :	· · · · :	· · · · :
	2		3	4
Rattles	* *

b

Leader	: -------	------- :	------- :	------- :
	a	b	a	b
Orchestra	: · · · ·	· · · · :	a Orch. Vars. :	· · · · :
	5		6	7
Rattles	* *

	a	b	a	b	
Orchestra	....	....	....	....	
Rattles	8 ******	******	9 ******	10 ******	
Orchestra	....	....	....	....	
Rattles	11 ******	******	12 ******	13 ******	
Orchestra	....	....	....	....	
Rattles	14 ******	******	15 ******	16 ******	
Leader	....	b	a	b	(mf) OM phrase
Orchestra	a	....	....	....	
Rattles	17 ******	******	18 ******	19 ******	a (f) OM sentence
Leader	....	b	a	b	
Orchestra	a	....	....	....	
Rattles	20 ******	******	21 ******	22 ******	

	(mf) OM phrase in ovs.	(f) OM sentence in ovs.

Leader   : b   : a   b   : a   a
Orchestra   a   b   a   b   a   b
                                      23   24   25
Rattles   *

Leader   :----------b----------:
Orchestra   a   b   a   b   a   b
                                      26   27   28
Rattles   *

                                       (f) Indication   (ff) *kuvelusa*
Leader   : b   : a   b   : a   a
Orchestra   a   b   a   b   a   b
                                      29   30   31
Rattles   *

Singers   S 1   (1) *Lavanani*......
                                                               :oooooooooooooooo:ooooooooooooo:ooo:
Leader   :   :   :   :   : a (p)   b
Orchestra   a   b   a (dim)   b
                                      32   33   34
Rattles   */ /

Singers	*Howotawa....* :oooooooooo:	:	$S\,\mathit{I}$	(1) *Lavanani......* :oooooooooooooo:oooooooooooo:ooo:	(2)
Leader	:	*Lavanani!* ooo:oooo	:	:	:
Treble Timbila } Orchestra	: a	: b	: a	‧‧‧‧‧‧‧‧ : b	: ....
	35		36	37	

Singers	:oooooooooo:	:	$S\,\mathit{I}$	(3) *Ŋguyusa.....* :ooooooooooooooo:ooooooo:	(4) :ooo:
Leader	:	*Ŋguyusa!* ooo:ooooooo	:	:	:
Treble Timbila } Orchestra	: a	: b	: a	‧‧‧‧‧‧‧‧ : b	: ....
	38		39	40	

Singers	*Nopwata.....* :ooooooo:	:	$S\,\mathit{I}$	(3) *Ŋguyusa.....* :ooooooooooooooo:ooooooo:	(4) :ooo:
Leader	:	*Ŋguyusa!* :ooo:oooo	:	:	:
Treble Timbila } Orchestra	: a	: b	: a	‧‧‧‧‧‧‧‧ : b	: ....
	41		42	43	

	44	45	46
Singers	*Nopwata...* :ooooooo:	:	:
Leader	: *A-konga ko!* :ooo:ooooooo	: a	: b
Orchestra	:	:	:
Treble Timbila } a	....	....	....
Orchestra	:	:	:

	47	48	49
Singers	(6) *A-konga ko...* :oooooooooooooo:	(7) *Kwalakanya...* :oooooooooo:oooooooooo	:
Leader	:	: *A-konga ko!* ooo:ooooooo	:
Treble Timbila } a	.... b	.... a	.... b
Orchestra	:	:	:

	50	51	52
Singers	S 2 (5) *A-konga ko....* :oooooooooooooo:	(6) *A-konga ko...* :ooooooooooooooo:	(7) *Kwalakanya...........* :oooooooooo:oooooooooo:
Leader	:	:	:
Treble Timbila } a	.... b	.... a	.... b
Orchestra	:	:	*Maninya!* :oooooooo

	S 3 (8) *Maninya*.........			(9) *Maninya*.........			(10) *Mane*.........	
Singers	:ooooooooooooooooo:ooooooo:	:	:	:oooooooooooooo:ooooooo:	:	:	:oooooo:oooooo:oooooo:oooooooooooooooo:	:
Leader	:	:	:	:	:	*Maninya!*	:	:
Treble Timbila	:	:	:	:	:	:oooooooo	:	:
	a	b	a	b	a		a	b
Orchestra	....	....	....	....	....		....	....
	53		54		55			
	(9) *Maninya*.........	(10) *Mane*.........	S 3 (8) *Maninya*.........			(9) *Maninya*.........		
Singers	:oooooooooooooooo:ooooooo:oooooo:oooooooooooooooo:	:oooooooooooooo:ooooooo:	:	:	:oooooooooooooo:oooooo:oooooo:oooooooooooooooo:	:
Leader	:	:	:	:	:	*Dabwa!*
Treble Timbila	:	:	:	:	:	:oooooo
	a	b	a	b	a	b
Orchestra	....	....	....	....	....	....
	56		57		58		59		60		61

Singers	:	*S 4* (11) *Dabwa....* (12) *Filipe.........* :oooooooooooooooo:ooooooo:	:
Leader	:	: *Dabwa!* : oooo:ooo	:
Treble ⎫ Timbila ⎬ Orchestra ⎭	:--:--:--:--:--: a b :............	a b :............	:
		62	63

Singers	:	*S 4* (11) *Dabwa....* (12) *Filipe.........* :oooooooooooooooo:ooooooo:	:
Leader	:	: *Awi Lakeni!* :oooooooooo	:
Treble ⎫ Timbila ⎬ Orchestra ⎭	:--:--:--:--:--: a b :............	a b :............	:
		65	66

Singers	:	*S 5* (13) *Awi Lakeni.......* :oooooooooooooo:ooooooo:	(14) *Awi Lakeni....* (15) O :oooooooooooooooo:oooooooo:ooooooo
Leader	:	:	:
Treble ⎫ Timbila ⎬ Orchestra ⎭	:--:--:--:--:--: a b :............	a b :............	:
		68	69 70

	O *upɣala*.....			S 5 (13) *Avi Lakeni*.......
Singers	:ooooooooooo:			:oooooooooooooooo:ooooooo:
Leader		*Avi Lakeni!*		
		ooo:ooooooo		
Treble Timbila }	:	: b	:	: b
	a		a	
Orchestra	....	....	....	....
	71	72	73	

	(14) *Avi Lakeni*...... (15) O *upɣala*.........			
Singers	:ooooooooooooooooo:ooooooo:ooooooo:ooooooo:			
Leader			*VaZandameleni!*	
			oooooo:ooooo	
Treble Timbila }	:	: b	:	: b
	a		a	
Orchestra	....	....	....	....
	74	75	76	

	S 4 (16) *VaZandameleni* (17) *Ŋgoŋgondo*......			
Singers	:ooooooooooooooo:oooooooooooooo:ooooooo:			
Leader			*VaZandameleni!*	
			ooooooo:ooooo	
Treble Timbila }	:	: b	:	: b
	a		a	
Orchestra	....	....	....	....
	77	78	79	

(16) *VaZandameleni* (17) *Ngoygondo*........

			Lavanani!		
Singers : ooooooooooooooo : ooooooooooooooo : ooooooo : : : :
Leader : : : : oooooooo : : :
            a   b   a   b
Orchestra ....
            80   81

Singers : : : : :
(f) Indication (ff) *kuvelusa*   a (ff) Presto
Leader ------------ : : : :
            a   b   a   b
Orchestra ....
            83   84   85
Rattles : : ************************************

Coda. *S I* (18) *Lavanani*..........

Singers : : : ooooooooooooooo : ooooooo : //
Leader : : : : //
            a   b   a   b
Orchestra .... : ********: //
            86   87
Rattles ************************************ //

BIBLIOGRAPHY

The Bibliography of the Chopi is very small, and in what is available only a few authors so much as mention their music. The most authoritative works in English are by the Junods and one or two short articles by Dora Earthy. I shall only enumerate those works which make direct reference, however brief, to our subject. For a more complete bibliography the reader is referred to the list given by H. P. Junod (to whom I am greatly indebted) in his introductory article on the Chopi to A. M. Duggan-Cronin's photographic studies in the series *The Bantu Tribes of South Africa*, vol. iv, section ii, 'The Vachopi of Portuguese East Africa'.

Reference to the Statistical Department at Lourenço Marques only revealed two articles on the subject written by Portuguese, one by Belo Marques already mentioned and the other by H. C. Bastos and C. Montez, neither of which unfortunately have I been able to obtain.

BASTOS, HENRIQUETA CALÇADE, and MONTEZ, C. 'Kossi N'Quaio—A grande festa do Rei Gungunhana', in *Moçambique*, No. 4, 1935. Imprensa Nacional de Moçambique.

DUGGAN-CRONIN, A. M. *The Bantu Tribes of South Africa*. Reproductions of photographic studies. 'The Vachopi of Portuguese East Africa', with an introductory article on the Vachopi by Henri-Philippe Junod, B.A., B.D., vol. iv, section ii, plates XLI–LXXX. Cambridge, 1936.

EARTHY, E. DORA. 'Some Agricultural Rites of Valenge and Vachopi' (continued). *Bantu Studies*, vol. ii, No. 4, October 1926. University of the Witwatersrand, Johannesburg.

ELSDON-DEW, RONALD, M.D. 'Blood Groups in Africa.' *The South African Institute for Medical Research*, No. XLIV (vol. ix, pp. 29–94). 1939.

—— 'African Ethnology, the Evidence of the Blood Groups.' *Primeiro Congresso Médico de Lourenço Marques*, vol. ii, pp. 15–21. Sept. 1938. Imprensa Nacional de Moçambique, 1941.

JUNOD, H. A. *The Life of a South African Tribe*. Neuchâtel, 1927, 2nd ed., 2 vols., 8vo. Vol. ii.

—— *Les Chants et les contes des Ba-Ronga, de la Baie de Delagoa*. Georges Bridel & Co., Lausanne, 1897.

JUNOD, HENRI-PHILIPPE. I. 'Some Notes on Tfopi Origins.' *Bantu Studies*, iii, 1927–9, pp. 57–70, map. (Geographical distribution and history.)

—— 'The Mbila or Native Piano of the Tfopi tribe.' *Bantu Studies*, iii, 1927–9, pp. 275–85. (A description of the Chopi xylophone under the headings: General, different kinds of timbila, making, customs connected with it, playing it.)

JUNOD, HENRI-PHILIPPE. *Éléments de grammaire tchopi*. Lisboa: Tipografia Carmona, 1931, pp. 43. (An elementary grammar of the Chopi language.)

—— 'Spécimens du folklore de la tribu des BaTchopi.' *Africa*, 1933, vi. 90–5.

KIRBY, P. R. *The Musical Instruments of the Native Races of South Africa*. Oxford, 1934. 4to. Pp. xix+285, 73 pls. (Pp. 57–65 describe Chopi xylophones and music.)

MARQUES, BELO. *Musica negra*. Ediçao da Agencia Geral das Colonias. 1943.

THEAL, G. M. *Records of South Eastern Africa*, vol. ii, pp. 62–150. Extracts from the Book called *Lendas da India*. (Extracts from the letters of Father André Fernandes, June 1560 and December 1562.)

TRACEY, HUGH T. 'Tres dias com os Bachope.' *Moçambique*, No. 24, 1940, Imprensa Nacional de Moçambique, pp. 23–58. (A preliminary impression of Chopi Orchestras.)

—— 'Musica, poesia e bailados chopes.' *Moçambique*, No. 30, 1942, pp. 69–112. (A study of the music and poetry of two Chopi orchestral dances, with comparative tunings of their scales.)

—— 'Marimbas, Os xilophones dos changanes.' *Moçambique*, No. 31, 1942, pp. 49–61. (Xylophones of the Shangaan-Ndau.)

—— 'The Poetry of the Bachopi Ballet.' *NADA*, no. 21, pp. 6–18. Salisbury, 1944. (Examples of poems from two *Migodo*.)

INDEX

absolute pitch, 137.
accidents: mining, 69, 71, 81.
Administrador, of Manhiça district, 127.
— of Zavala district, 13, 17, 18, 20, 22, 36, 44, 45, 50, 56, 69, 97, 127, 134, 143.
Alexander's Rag-time Band, 34.
analysis of *Mzeno* movement, 161 ff.
ancestor worship, 45.
ancestors, 45.
ancestral spirit, 95.
arena, *see* dance arena.
armlet, 85.
aural music, 107.

Bach, 7.
ballet, 45, 52, 85, 110.
banana plantations, 35, 49.
bangles, 58, 59.
Banguza, district and village of, 2, 30, 33, 36, 37, 38, 45, 49, 59, 126, 129.
— Chief, *see* Filippe we Mudumane.
Bantu, ix, 4, 33, 44, 52, 75, 84, 93.
— languages, 8, 67 n.
beaters, 5, 38, 77, 99, 108, 129, 140, 141, 142.
beer, 70.
Beethoven, 7.
blind leader, 124.
blood grouping, 123.
Blunt, Mr. M. F., Portuguese Consul, x.
book, taxation, 50.
Boone, Olga, 118.
bottle, 48, 49, 102.
Brahms, 7.
Brazil, 118.
bribes, 31.
Bulafu, maker of *timbila*, 123, 127.
bullock tail, 85.

cadenza, 6, 91, 92, 96, 98, 99, 100, 110, 121.
cage (of mine), 68, 72.
cashew nut, 12 ff., 42, 51, 70.
cathartic function of African music, 3.
cazhu, *see* cashew.
centenary celebrations, 126.
chaconne, 7, 162.
Chamosi, son of Sauli Ilova, 55, 57.
Chamusi, office of W.N.L.A., 48, 50.
Chichopi, 4, 9, 23, 30.
chieftainship, 25, 45, 56, 65, 69, 74, 98.
Chigomba Mavila, *see* Mavila.
children's dances, 77, 119.
Chilenguni (Johannesburg), 80.
Chilenji, 69, 71.

Chimuke (Administrador), 17.
Chisiko, Chief Chugela, 69, 70.
— village and district, 55, 57, 69, 72, 76, 88.
Chitombe, tribal ancestor, 20.
Chopi language, *see* Chichopi.
— people, 1, 2, 9, 16, 20, 21, 23, 31, 34, 36, 37, 43, 64, 71, 75, 80, 110, 111, 116, 141.
Chugela, *see* Chisiko, Chief.
cicatrices, 33, 58, 85.
cider, 12 ff., 42, 51, 67, 70, 87.
civet-skin, 85.
cloth, 46, 85, 116.
clothes, 37, 46, 85.
clowns, 88.
coda, 5, 6, 90, 94, 109, 162, 163.
compensation, 71, 81.
competition, 33, 112.
composer, 2, 4, 5, 6, 107, 110, 113, 114.
composition (of verse and music), 2 ff., 5, 35, 113, 125.
compound manager, 31, 82, 112, 115.
conductor, 109.
Congo, 118.
contra-melody, *see* melody.
conversation, 59.
corporal punishment, 15, 48, 50.
Corrientes, Cape, 2, 51, 118, 143.
court (magistrates'), 35, 48.
craftsmen, 126, 129.
cries, 27, 75, 82, 95, 99, 103.
Cruddas, W. G., 86.
curing (of wood), 135 ff.
Customs authorities, 115.

dance, 1, 2, 4, 6, 7, 77, 84 ff., 106, 146.
— arena, 112.
— (children's), 77, 119.
— competition, 112.
— days, 49, 97.
— floor, 9, 77, 95, 100, 112.
— leader, 6, 86 ff., 92, 94, 100, 103, 104, 116.
— rhythm, 9.
— routine, 6, 86, 101, 103, 109, 116, 161, 162, 163.
— stick, 85, 102, 104.
— terms, 152, 153.
dancers, 6, 32, 38, 40, 51, 53, 66, 77, 84 ff., 116, 118, 149, 162, 163.
dancing, ix, 86, 87, 112, 117.
Darule, Chief's messenger, 65.
Davida, Chief at Manhiça, 127.
Dawoti, clerk at Administrador's office, 20, 21, 48, 50, 91.

INDEX

decorations, 85.
Delagoa Bay, 65, 74.
devil, 87.
dialects (Chopi), 9, 66.
discord, 58.
distribution of notes of *timbila*, 120.
diviner, 30, 62, 64, 72.
division (word), 10.
doctor, *see* herbalist.
drink, 17, 36, 49, 68, 70, 143, 145, 146.
drums, 38, 40, 52, 97, 99, 100, 143, 146.
Durban, visit of Chopi musicians to, 2, 27, 33, 86, 97, 104, 126.
dust, 87.
Dutch, 81.

eggs, 10, 11.
elders, 80, 103.
elephant, 62, 68, 71.
Ellis, H. J., 125.
English names, 38, 47, 64.
— people, 81.
— pound, 10, 11.
ensemble, of instruments, 119, 142.
Europe, 124, 126.
European clothes, 85.
— melodies, 116.
Europeans, 10, 14, 45, 87, 88, 106, 126, 128, 141, 161.
exhibition, 126.

Fambanyane, 18, 19.
farm, *see* banana plantation.
Fernandes, Father André, 18, 51, 70, 86, 87, 93, 110, 117, 119, 137, 139, 141, 143 ff.
Figueiredo, Captain Antonio, x.
Filippe we Mudumane (Mindumane), 2, 17, 29, 33, 36, 39, 41, 45, 49, 59, 75, 97, 114, 126.
films, 88.
first aid, 85.
food, 48, 51, 143.
Fortini (dancer), 64.
Froes, Luiz, 145.

gala performance, 112.
Gamba, Chief, 143, 145.
Germans, 22, 46, 48, 80, 146.
Germiston (Transvaal), 79.
Gilbert and Sullivan, 4, 45.
goat, 67.
— skin, 85, 116.
god (tribal), 95.
'God save the King', 116.
Gomukomu, orchestra leader, x, 2, 4, 29, 33, 35, 36, 39, 42, 44, 46, 49, 50, 52, 76, 84, 88, 97, 98, 100, 101, 102, 103, 108, 114, 119, 161.
'good-bye', custom of saying, 27.

gourd, 131 ff., 139, 140, 145.
gramophone, *see* records.
guild of craftsmen, 37.
Gungunyana (Ngungunyana), 75.
Gusikov (Russian xylophonist), 107, 108.
Gwambini, Chief, 134.

Hallett, L. G., x, 112.
hallmark, 132.
hand beating, *see* corporal punishment.
hand pianos, see *mbira*.
harmony, 101.
heptatonic scale, 118, 128.
herbalist, 73, 118.
hexatonic scale, 122.
hippopotamus skull, 98.
history (tribal), 122.
H.M.V. Gramophone Company, 36.
Hombe, 119, 124, 126, 127, 137, 138.
home music, 128.
horse tail, 85.
hospitality, 80.

igodo, see *ŋgodo*.
impresario, 92.
Incomati River (Inkomati), 1, 21, 75, 127.
indication (by leading player), 6, 90, 99, 100, 162.
Inhambane, 2, 50, 143.
Inharrime, 51, 134.
inheritance, 20, 38, 45.
inspiration, 76.
integrity (musical), 125.
Italians, 80.

jackal-skin, 52, 85, 90, 116.
jail, 57, 78, 79.
Johannesburg, 2, 36, 59, 80, 85.
Julai, head sepoy, 48, 50.
junior *ŋgodo*, 77, 83.
Junod, Rev. H. P., x, 134.

Kaffir, 145.
— beer, 70.
— orange tree, 131.
Kapitini, Chief's messenger, 12, 13, 24.
Karanga people, 8, 14, 107, 123, 137.
Katini, orchestra leader, x, 2, 4, 10, 12, 13, 17, 19, 22, 24, 27, 44, 50, 75, 88, 90, 91, 92, 95, 108, 114, 119, 123, 126, 127, 128, 129, 135.
Kawane, sister of Gomukomu, 44, 45.
key-note, 98.
'king's note', 124.
Kirby, P. R., 121 n.
Komichi, dance leader, 92, 94, 96.

lake, 49, 55, 59, 69, 117.

INDEX

Lakeni, Administrador's messenger, 36, 41, 42.
lament, 55, 57, 69.
law (tribal), 20.
leader, of dancers, 85, 116.
— of orchestra, 110, 113, 121, 123, 163.
leadership, of Chiefs, 37, 76.
learning the *timbila*, 108.
left-handed players, 136, 141.
leggings, 85, 90, 116.
leitmotive, 5, 161.
Limpopo River, ix, 1, 16, 46, 75.
lion (musician), 79.
Lisbon, 26, 27, 126.
Lourenço Marques, ix, 27, 65, 74, 80.
luck, 30.
lyric, 3, 4, 6, 8 ff., 52, 59, 84, 162.

Madikise, 20, 22.
Madoshimani, 2.
mafureira tree, 130, 131.
Magul, 21, 23, 51, 75, 126, 127.
Mahamba, Cabo, 133.
Mahlabezulu, brother of Gomukomu, 36, 49.
mails, *see* post.
Majanyana, instrument maker and translator, x, 2, 37, 63, 69, 72, 129.
Makatachilo village, 64.
makers of *timbila*, see *timbila*.
malimba, 118.
malingerer, 82.
Mangachilo, Cabo, 133.
Mangeni (Mangene), 2, 17, 33, 37, 38.
Mangomanyani, composer, 80.
Manhiça, village and district, ix, 1, 127.
Manjacaze, district, 50.
Manjengwe (musician), 18, 22, 25, 26, 27, 50, 63.
manufacture of *timbila*, see *timbila*.
marimba, see *malimba*.
Marques, Sn. Belo, ix
Mashewani, wife of Katini, 13.
Masinga, K. E., x.
Matijawo (dancer), 47, 48.
Matikiti, 54, 55, 56, 57, 60.
Matuwane, 68, 69.
Mavila, Chief Chigomba, 52, 54, 56, 60, 64, 65.
Mavulendhlovu, 75.
Mawawana, country of Chisiko q.v.
mbira (hand pianos), 118, 122, 123, 137.
melodies, European, 116.
melody, 5, 7, 9, 101, 102, 109, 161.
contra m., 5, 7, 109.
mendelian dominant, 123.
mendicant, 37.
Meneti Nzekani, 77.
microphone, 106.
migodo, see *ŋgodo*.

military exercises, 86.
mime, 102.
Mindumane, Chief, 17.
mines, *see* Rand Mines.
mirrors, 85.
missionaries, 87, 143.
·mobility, 127.
Moçambique Territory, 11, 21, 34, 123.
Mocaranga, kingdom and people of, 71, 137, 144.
modality, 107.
money, exchange of, 11.
monkey skins, 85.
— -nuts, 69.
Monomotapa, kingdom of, 122, 137.
monotony (of foreign music), 86.
Montanha, Captain Furtado, x.
Montez, Lt. Caetano de Carvalho, x.
moral effect (of music), 29.
motion pictures, 88.
mourning, 55, 68.
msaho, 33.
Muchopes, district of, 50.
mukusu trees, 35, 97, 130.
mulatto, 71.
Musée du Congo Belge, 118.
music, African, cathartic function of, 3.
— seventeenth-century, 7.
musical terms, 124, 149 ff.
musician (travelling), 37.
musicians, *see* players.
musicology, 107.
Mwazikingi (Masikinki), 78, 79.
mwenje trees, 133, 134, 135.
— wood, 115, 129, 136.

names, English, 38, 47.
— native, 71.
— of notes, 107, 120, 121.
— of persons and places, 8.
— Portuguese, 38.
— writing of, 35.
National Anthem, Portuguese, 96, 116.
national music, 114, 117.
Native Commissioner, *see* Administrador.
Ndau people, 118, 122.
ŋgodo, 1, 4, 7, 9, 10, 15, 17, 19, 22, 24, 26, 27, 29, 35, 37, 39, 44, 50, 52, 63, 66, 76, 77, 83, 85, 88, 89, 90, 96, 97, 98, 105, 106, 114, 116, 118, 119, 134, 143, 149, 154, 161.
Ngongondo, Chief, of Zandamela district, 36.
Ngungundwane, former Administrador, 22, 48, 50.
Ngungunyana, *see* Gungunyana.
Nguyusa, brother of Gomukomu, 35, 36, 49.
njari, 123.

INDEX

Nkanda, *see* Nyakutowa.
notation, 107, 161.
notes (of *timbila*), 107, 119, 121, 136, 139.
Nyabindini, village and Chief, 24, 27, 48, 49.
Nyakutowa, district and village, 49, 64, 124, 143.

octave, 90, 99, 119, 122, 126, 138, 142.
office of Administrador, 49, 50, 69, 80.
old men dancing, 84.
onomatopoeic words, 67 n.
orchestra of *timbila*, 1, 32, 49, 89 ff., 100, 104, 109, 112, 118, 127.
orchestral ground, 54, 162.
— motive, 101, 109, 162.
— movement, analysis of, 161 ff.
originality, 65.
Otongue, 144.
Oxford Companion to Music, 7, 126, 137 n., 161 n.

passacaglia, 7, 162.
patronage, 117.
pentatonic scale, 118.
percussion, 7.
physique, 84.
piano, pianino, see *mbira*.
pipes (*chimveke*), 77.
pitch, 5, 114, 122, 124, 126, 128, 137.
  absolute p., 137.
  standard p., 114, 115, 126.
players, 106 ff.
poems, 3, 9.
poet, 71.
poetic terms, 8.
poetry, ix, 4, 5, 7, 8, 9, 32, 52, 75, 76, 102, 113, 117, 143.
poison, 60.
polygamy, 42.
Portugal, 126.
Portuguese consul, Durban, x.
— East Africa, 1, 31, 115.
— Government, 22, 74.
— people and affairs, 10, 14, 15, 21, 48, 74, 80, 81, 143, 145.
'possum', 62, 63.
post, 70, 71.
poverty, 62.
President of Portugal, 21, 23, 51, 126, 127.
Pretoria, 80.
prison, *see* jail.
Pritchett, V. S., 4.
psycho-physical norm, 123.
publication, of music and poetry, 106, 128.
Pungwe River, 137.

Quissico, Chief and district, *see* Chisiko.
— village, headquarters of the Administrador of the Zavala District, 27, 49, 57, 64, 69, 123.
Quiteve, chief, 137.

railway, 115, 116.
Rand gold mines, 11, 31, 34, 38, 41, 46, 49, 60, 68, 76, 79, 80, 111, 119, 121, 128.
rattle, 93, 163, 164.
— players, 89, 94, 102, 163.
recording, 102, 106, 109, 162.
records, gramophone, 36, 106, 116, 128.
recruiting officer, 60.
Reef, 2, 80, 112, 114, 115, 127, 139.
repetition in Chopi verse, 5.
research, 88, 122.
resonators, 115, 129, 130 ff., 138 ff.
Rhodesia, Southern, 86, 122, 137.
rice, 63.
right of way, 32, 33.
Rose Deep Mine, 23.
royal greeting, 78, 103.
— houses, chieftains, 44, 45.
rubber, and rubber tree, 141, 142.

Sabi River, 118.
sand, 93.
Santos, João dos, 137, 142 n.
'Sarie Marais', 116.
Sauli Ilova, leader of orchestra, 52, 53, 60, 65.
scale, 58, 107, 108, 114, 115, 121, 123, 124, 125, 127, 128, 138.
Scholes, Percy, 7, 126 n.
science of music, 129.
'Scotchmen', Chopi dancers, 81, 82.
semitic, 52.
sepoy, native police, 15, 50.
Sewe, *see* Inhambane.
Shangaan people, 16, 17, 21, 23, 31, 52, 75, 86, 95, 122.
Shangana-Ndau people, 118, 122.
shield, 85, 91, 93, 94, 96, 100, 104.
Shilenguni, 82.
Shona people, 137.
Sibuyeye, 16, 17.
Silveira, Father Gonzalo de, 86, 87, 145.
Simmer and Jack Mine, 113.
'sinews', 141, 142.
Sipingani Likwekwe, leader of orchestra, 66, 69, 70, 71, 75.
Sitwell, Sacheverell, 107.
slave, Tonga, 74.
slaves, 118.
sneezewood, see *mwenje*.
solo dance, 27, 98.
— instrument, 119.

INDEX

solo pieces, 119.
soloist, 109.
songs, words of African, 8.
Sotho people, 23, 30, 52.
South Africans, 80.
— America, 118.
Southern Rhodesia, see Rhodesia.
spears, 91, 94, 100, 104.
spectators, 93, 101.
spirit nursery, 45.
standard pitch, 114, 115.
Statistical Department, Lourenço Marques, 81 n.
stick (dance), 84, 85, 94, 100, 104.
stores, Indian, 46, 70.
— Portuguese, 70.
subject (musical), 6, 164.
submarines, 80.
succession, of chiefs, 18, 20, 25, 69, 74.
sugar estates, 35.
Sullivan (Gilbert and S.), 4.
swaying movement, 91, 92, 100, 101.

tablature, 161, 163, 165 ff.
tax on wood-cutting, 134, 135.
taxes, 10, 44, 113.
'Tea for Two', 116.
temperament, 124.
Tercentenary Celebrations, Lisbon, 26.
Theal, G. M., 137 n., 142 n.
theatre, 49.
Thornycroft, railway bus, 49.
timbila, Chopi xylophone, 1, 5, 12, 13, 16, 25, 32, 33, 37, 46, 48, 49, 74, 90, 92, 93, 97, 103, 108, 112, 115, 118 ff., 127, 128.
— makers of, 123, 129, 134, 142.
— manufacture of, 129 ff.
— music, 43, 52.
— practice *t.*, 77.
— range of, 119, 121.
— tone of, 93, 124, 139, 140.
— tuning of, 121, 125, 129, 136, 137, 140, 142.
toadstool, 60.
tonality, 59, 107, 114, 121.
Tonga people, 65, 80.
tonic, 96, 123, 124, 126, 127, 128, 137.
tools, 128.
training to dance and play, 77.
trance, 4, 87.
Transvaal, 95, 113.
treble variation, 162.
trousers, 48, 50, 65.
trumpets, 139, 140, 145.
tuning, 121 ff.
— forks, 122, 128, 137.
Twelfu, 113, 114.

uniform, worn by chiefs, 21, 22, 68.
unison, 6, 88, 92, 95, 96, 99, 104, 109.

variations on basic melody, 5, 6, 32, 86, 101, 109, 161, 162.
Vasconcelos, Dr. Luiz de V., x, 20, 143.
Venda people, 59.
verses, 2.
vibrator, 139, 140.
Village Main Mine, 114.
village music, 76, 113, 114, 117.
Vinichi, humorist, 67.
virtuosity, 107, 121.
vocal indication, see indication.

wages, 110.
Wanzileni, people of Zavala or Zileni, 74.
war, European, 22, 34, 48, 80.
— native, 75, 87.
'war dances', 87.
'warriors', 87.
Watussi people, 52.
West Africa, 220.
wiping faces of players or dancers, 77, 101.
Witwatersrand, 80, 111, 160.
— Deep Mine, 79, 145.
— Native Labour Association, 49, 60, 160.
wizards, 146.
W.N.L.A., see Witwatersrand Native Labour Association.
women, dancing and parading, 93, 99.
word-endings, 8.

Xhosa people, 30, 85.
xylophones, 1, 13, 26, 37, 118, 119, 121, 134, 163.
xylophonist (Russian), 107, 108, 141.

Zambesi River, ix, 36, 118.
Zandamela, Chief and district, 64, 84, 85, 124, 126, 129, 133, 134.
Zavala, Blande, brother of Wani, 114.
— District, 1, 10, 18, 26, 52, 88, 115, 123, 127, 128.
— Wani, Paramount Chief, 2, 8, 13, 17, 18, 26, 27, 28, 50, 70, 90.
Zulu dance, 86.
— people, 8, 31, 33, 52, 59, 85, 114.
— poetry, 9.
— tribal loyalty, 17.
Zululand, 33.